MEDIAEVAL SOURCES
IN TRANSLATION

3

St. Thomas Aquinas

THE DIVISION AND METHODS
OF THE SCIENCES

Questions v and vi of his Commentary
on the *De Trinitate* of Boethius
translated with Introduction
and Notes

Fourth Revised Edition

by

ARMAND MAURER

PONTIFICAL INSTITUTE
OF MEDIAEVAL STUDIES

LIBRARY OF CONGRESS CATALOGUING DATA (Revised)

Thomas Aquinas, Saint, 1225?-1274.

The division and methods of the sciences. Questions V and VI of his Commentary on the *De Trinitate* of Boethius, translated with introd. and notes, by Armand Maurer. 4th rev. ed. [Toronto], Pontifical Institute of Mediaeval Studies, [c1986, 1953].

(Mediaeval sources in translation ; 3 ISSN 0316-0874)
Bibliography: p.
Includes index.
ISBN 0-88844-279-3

1. Classification of sciences.   2. Boethius, d. 524. De Trinitate.   I. Maurer, Armand Augustine, 1915-, ed. and tr.   II. Pontifical Institute of Mediaeval Studies.   III. Title.   IV. Series.

BD240.T52   1985

PRINTED BY UNIVERSA, WETTEREN, BELGIUM

Distributed outside North America by
E. J. Brill, Postbus 9000,
2300 PA Leiden, The Netherlands
E. J. Brill, ISBN: 90 04 07932 7

Contents

Abbreviations

CCL   Corpus Christianorum, series latina
CSEL Corpus scriptorum ecclesiasticorum latinorum
PG   Migne, Patrologia graeca
PL   Migne, Patrologia latina

Introduction

I

St. Thomas Aquinas gives his views on the hierarchy of the sciences and their methods in several of his works, but his most extensive and penetrating treatment of these subjects is to be found in the two Questions translated in this little book. They are taken from his unfinished Commentary on Boethius' *De Trinitate*. Question Five deals with the division of the speculative sciences, Question Six with their methods. The Questions were written early in St. Thomas' career, very likely between 1255 and 1259,[1] so that they are not always his last word on the subject; what he says in them should be studied along with his statements in his later works. Yet, because he never again took up the problems in such detail, they are of exceptional value in giving us an appreciation of his views on these topics.

It may appear strange that St. Thomas treats of the division and methods of the sciences while commenting on Boethius' book on the Trinity. However, he is simply taking his cue from Boethius himself, who, before considering the mystery of the Trinity, touches upon certain preliminary points concerning faith, theology, and the place of theology in the scheme of the sciences. A few brief remarks of

---

[1] See B. Decker, *Sancti Thomae de Aquino. Expositio super librum Boethii De Trinitate*, p. 44; M. D. Chenu, "La date du commentaire de saint Thomas sur le *De Trinitate* de Boèce," *Revue des sciences philosophiques et théologiques* 30 (1941-1942), 432-434.

Boethius about the division of the speculative sciences and their methods of procedure form the basis of St. Thomas' lengthy discussions on these points.[2]

The circumstance of the Commentary also helps to explain the limited perspective of St. Thomas in the two Questions. In the first place, they are concerned specifically with the speculative and not with the practical sciences. It is true that he has some important things to say in them about practical knowledge and science, but these are incidental to his main theme. They are simply meant to throw more light on the nature of speculative science. No attempt is made to give the hierarchy of practical science.[3]

Moreover, the nature of theology as the science of Sacred Scripture is not considered in these Questions. They contain a few incidental remarks about it, but these are only to contrast it with metaphysics. St. Thomas had already treated of the science of Sacred Scripture in the earlier Questions (I-III). Here his perspective is that of the sciences attainable through the natural light of reason.

In order to appreciate the aim and significance of the present work, the reader must understand St. Thomas' notion of science. It will be apparent at once that it differs significantly from that current in our own day. The very fact that he uses the terms *science* and *philosophy* as synonyms warns us of this and at the same time points to his ideal of science. Today, no one would think of equating philosophy and science, even though there is little agreement as to what the distinction between them is. Science in general is thought of as any reasoned knowledge that is universal and systematic. The ideal scientific knowledge is to be found in an exact science such as

---

[2] See Boethius, *De Trinitate* 2, below, pp. 3-4.
[3] On this subject, see J. Maritain, *The Degrees of Knowledge*, pp. 311-316, and Appendix VII, pp. 456-464.

mathematical physics, which uses precise mathematical calculations and a highly refined method involving experimentation, formation of hypotheses and their verification. Whatever philosophy may be, it obviously does not fit this description.

St. Thomas' ideal of science is quite different.[4] For him, science in general is knowledge of things through their causes.[5] As Aristotle said before him, it is knowledge not only of fact, but of reasoned fact.[6] It reaches its ideal, not simply when it records observable connections in nature and calculates them in mathematical terms, but rather when it accounts for observable phenomena and the properties of things by bringing to light their intelligible relations to their causes. Metaphysics reaches this goal when, for example, it explains the contingent universe through God, mathematics when it explains the properties of a triangle through its definition, natural philosophy when it accounts for change through efficient and final causes and the intrinsic principles of bodies, matter and form.

---

[4] For background studies in science in the Middle Ages, see J. Mariétan, *Problème de la classification des sciences d'Aristote à s. Thomas;* P. Duhem, *Le système du monde. Histoire des doctrines cosmologiques de Platon à Copernic;* C. H. Haskins, *Studies in the History of Medieval Science;* G. Sarton, *Introduction to the History of Science;* A. C. Crombie, *Augustine to Galileo. The History of Science A.D. 400-1650,* revised edition: *Medieval and Early Modern Science.* I. *Science in the Middle Ages: V-XIII Centuries,* II. *Science in the Later Middle Ages and Early Modern Times XIII-XVII Centuries;* J. A. Weisheipl, *The Development of Physical Theory in the Middle Ages;* idem, "Classification of the Sciences in Medieval Thought," *Mediaeval Studies* 27 (1965), 54-90; idem, *Nature and Gravitation;* W. A. Wallace, *Causality and Scientific Explanation,* I. *Medieval and Early Classical Sciences;* E. Grant (ed.), *A Source Book in Medieval Science;* D. C. Lindberg (ed.), *Sciences in the Middle Ages;* L. D. Roberts (ed.), *Approaches to Nature in the Middle Ages;* E. A. Moody, *Studies in Medieval Philosophy, Science, and Logic;* P. Kibre, *Studies in Medieval Science: Alchemy, Astrology, Mathematics, and Medicine.*

[5] See *In I Post Anal.* lect. 4, ed. Leonine, pp. 149-155; lect. 13, pp. 229-232.

[6] See *Posterior Analytics* 1.2, 71b8-72b4; 1.13.

In other words, scientific inquiry for St. Thomas at its best is philosophical. It does not aim simply at empiriological knowledge gained through controlled observation and measurement of the physical world, but rather at knowledge of the very being and essential structure of things. Its goal is *ontological* rather than *empiriological knowledge.*[7]

---

[7] For a further explanation of the meaning of these terms, see J. Maritain, *Philosophy of Nature*, pp. 73ff. See also his *The Degrees of Knowledge*, pp. 21-67, 136-201, and *Science and Wisdom*, pp. 3-69 as well as S. L. Jaki, "Maritain and Science," *The New Scholasticism* 58 (1984), 267-292.

The growth in modern times of empiriological science, as distinct from philosophy in its formal object and method, renders impossible a physical theory that would be applicable in a univocal way to both. Such a theory, which denies the distinction between philosophical and empiriological analysis, has been proposed by R. Nogar, "Toward a Physical Theory," *The New Scholasticism* 25 (1951), 397-438.

J. Weisheipl proposes a return to St. Thomas and St. Albert for "a unifying physical theory" that would include both the philosophy of nature and the empirical or experimental sciences. For Weisheipl these constitute one specific discipline, both materially and formally. However, he regards the sciences employing mathematical principles as really distinct from natural philosophy. See J. Weisheipl, *The Development of Physical Theory in the Middle Ages*; "The Relationship of Medieval Natural Philosophy to Modern Science: The Contribution of Thomas Aquinas to Its Understanding," in *Science, Medicine and the Universities 1200-1550. Essays in Honor of Pearl Kibre* (= *Manuscripta* 20 [1976]), pp. 181-196; idem, Introduction to *The Dignity of Science. Studies in the Philosophy of Science Presented to William Humbert Kane OP* (= *The Thomist* 24 [1961]).

In the same spirit, see C. De Koninck, "The Unity and Diversity of Natural Science," in *The Philosophy of Physics*, ed. V. E. Smith, pp. 5-24; W. A. Wallace, "St. Thomas's Conception of Natural Philosophy and its Method," in *Studi Tomistici. La philosophie de la nature de saint Thomas d'Aquin*, ed. L. Elders, pp. 7-27; idem, *Causality and Scientific Explanation*.

For further discussions of this topic, see E. McMullin, "Philosophies of Nature," *The New Scholasticism* 43 (1969), 29-74; J. Compton, "Reinventing the Philosophy of Nature," *The Review of Metaphysics* 33 (1979), 3-28; E. McMullin, "Compton on the Philosophy of Nature," ibid., pp. 29-58; idem, "Is There a Philosophy of Nature?" *Proceedings of the International Congress of Philosophy*, Vienna, 1968, 4: 295-305.

It is true that St. Thomas was acquainted with genuine empiriological inquiry, although its range was very limited and its methods
remained simple and undeveloped. During his lifetime, St. Albert
the Great carried out observations in biology and zoology which still
evoke the admiration of the scientist, Peter of Maricourt wrote his
treatise on the magnet, and Roger Bacon observed and measured the
rainbow and other phenomena of light.[8] It is not surprising, then, to
find St. Thomas' description of the method of natural science quite
correctly laying stress on the role of the senses in such knowledge,
on the verification of its judgments in sense data, and on reasoning
from signs and effects to causes.[9] What is more, he gives us the best
analysis of physico-mathematical science written in the Middle Ages.
He knew of this type of science in a very rudimentary form from the
ancients and also from his contemporaries, such as Robert Grosseteste, Roger Bacon, and Witelo, who cultivated it chiefly in the
field of astronomy and the mathematical study of light (optics). He
calls these *intermediary sciences* because they are situated between
mathematics and physics and partake of the character of both.[10]
Sciences of this sort, however, remained largely undeveloped in the
Middle Ages and their method was not adequately understood. They
play a very minor role in St. Thomas' scheme of the sciences.

[8] See G. Sarton, *Introduction to the History of Science*, vol. 2: for St. Albert,
pp. 934-944; for Peter of Maricourt (Petrus Peregrinus), pp. 1030-1032; for Roger
Bacon, pp. 952-967. St. Albert's emphasis on personal observation in the sciences
is particularly worthy of note. He writes: "What I have to say (on the various plant
species) is partly proven by experience (*experimento*), and partly taken from the
reports of those whom I have discovered do not readily make statements that are
not proven by experience." *De Vegetabilibus et Plantis* 6.1.1, ed. A. Borgnet (Paris,
1891), 10: 159-160.

[9] See below, pp. 66, 75.

[10] See below, pp. 43-45.

The center of attraction for St. Thomas and his contemporaries was not empiriological or mathematical science, but rather ontological or philosophical knowledge, which attains the very being and intelligible structure of things. Indeed, so great was the attraction toward this type of knowledge in the Middle Ages that the other sciences suffered from it. Not only did they fail to flourish and to achieve their independence as distinct kinds of knowledge, but all too frequently problems that can be solved only by their methods were approached with the methods of ontological science or philosophy. In general there was too great an optimism in the mind's ability to understand the ontological structure of things or their intelligible natures. The consequence of this optimism was the extension of philosophical analysis to areas in which it fails to achieve results. We know all too well the consequences of this; the corpse of mediaeval physics is there to warn us against the error.[11]

The beginning of the modern era witnessed a revolt against the physics of the Middle Ages. The empiriological and physico-mathematical sciences gradually established themselves as distinct scientific ways of knowing and their scope and methods were carefully defined. At first these sciences were taken as a substitute for the natural philosophy of the Middle Ages. Newton, for example, called his monumental work "The Mathematical Principles of Natural Philosophy." It was only much later, indeed within the last century,

---

[11] Mediaeval physics included parts that properly belong to the philosophy of nature and parts that belong to the science of nature. I am here referring to the latter and not to the former, at least insofar as they were not contaminated by incorrect science. The analysis of changeable beings in terms of form and matter, and of change itself in terms of act and potency, are examples of a sound philosophical explanation of nature. On the other hand, the mediaeval attempt to explain the particular movements in nature through tendencies toward natural places (see Q. 5, a. 2, note 25) is an instance of the misuse of the philosophic method in the domain of science.

that their non-philosophical character has been clearly recognized. This clarification not only benefits the scientist, who no longer takes his work to be a philosophical one, but it also helps the philosopher to appreciate better the limits of his own discipline. As a result, he too benefits from the separation of science from philosophy.

The tragedy was that the revolt against mediaeval physics was aimed not only at the bad physics of the Middle Ages, but against philosophy itself.[12] The methods of the sciences of controlled observation and measurement were hailed as the only ones that enable us to understand man and the universe. The method of ontological analysis, proper to philosophy, was denied all validity. The advent of positivism, with its repudiation of any ontological implication in science and its glorification of the positive sciences as the only valid method of knowing, gave these notions definitive form and fixed them indelibly in the modern mind. It should be added, however, that a reaction to positivism began as early as the nineteenth century, led by such philosophers as Emile Meyerson[13] and Edmund Husserl, the founder of phenomenology.

With positivism the modern world had its revenge on the Middle Ages, but not without itself suffering a loss. For if the methods of empiriological science are successful in dealing with many problems about the physical universe, they are equally unsuccessful in handling many others, and these indeed the most important of all, such as the very intelligibility of the universe, the nature of man, his ultimate origin and destiny, good and evil, and God. In fact, the methods of these sciences do not even enable us to investigate the meaning and value of science itself, and to evaluate the various types of knowledge and science.

---

[12] See J. Maritain, *Philosophy of Nature*, pp. 41ff.: "The Conflict of Methods at the End of the Middle Ages," *The Thomist* 3 (1941), 527-538.

[13] See his *De l'Explication dans les sciences.*

There is need, then, for a better understanding and appreciation of the ontological or philosophical method of knowing. And it is just for this reason that the philosophy of St. Thomas, and the present work in particular, are well worth our attention today. His analysis of the hierarchy of the sciences and of their methods is itself an excellent example of the ontological method. It is not his aim to draw up a detailed and complete classification of the sciences, but rather to exhibit the main divisions of the sciences known in his day in the light of the causes, both on the side of the object and on the side of the subject, which give rise to them. In fine, his inquiry is a strictly philosophical one. The product of an age quite different from our own, it does not always give us ready-made answers to our problems. St. Thomas knew nothing about our new types of science, and so his analysis of the sciences and their methods could not take them into account. But he sets before us a model of how such an analysis should be made, as well as the broad principles of being and knowing which, because they are true, are as relevant today as they were in his century.

II

In this brief Introduction[1] it would be impossible to comment on all the topics considered in these Questions and the many problems they raise. The topics include such important ones as logic,[1a] the

---

[1] The following historical and doctrinal studies of these Questions are especially recommended: L. Elders, *Faith and Science. An Introduction to St. Thomas'* Expositio in Boethii De Trinitate, pp. 85-140; S. Neumann, *Gegenstand und Methode der theoretischen Wissenschaften nach Thomas von Aquin auf Grund der* Expositio super librum Boethii De Trinitate.

[1a] See below, Q. 5, a. 1, Reply to 2 and 3, pp. 16-18.

liberal arts,[2] ethics,[3] practical science in general,[4] the subalternation of science,[5] and intermediate science.[6] Here we will confine our remarks to the two central themes of the Angelic Doctor: the hierarchy of the speculative sciences and their methods.

St. Thomas divides these sciences into three branches: natural philosophy or science, mathematics, and theology or divine science. It will be noticed that he uses the terms *natural science, physics,* and *natural philosophy* as synonyms. Like all ancient and mediaeval philosophers, he makes no distinction between them.[7] By *theology* is here meant first philosophy or metaphysics, not theology in the sense of the science of Sacred Scripture.[8]

This threefold division of the speculative sciences stems from Aristotle.[9] It was handed down to the Middle Ages by Boethius and adopted by St. Thomas. Each of these sciences is defined by its subject of inquiry and by its method of procedure. St. Thomas followed Boethius on this point too, but not without significant additions and alterations. According to Boethius, the sciences are concerned with *forms,* and the hierarchy of the sciences corresponds exactly to the hierarchy of forms in the real world in various degrees of separation from matter. Thus natural science studies the forms of

---

[2] Ibid., Reply to 3, pp. 17-19.

[3] Ibid.

[4] Ibid., Reply to 4, pp. 20-21.

[5] Ibid., Reply to 5, pp. 21-22.

[6] See below, Q. 5, a. 3, Reply to 6 and 7, pp. 44-45.

[7] Indeed, as late as the nineteenth century books in physics were called treatises on natural philosophy. Since then, the scope and method of science in the modern sense have been more clearly distinguished from those of natural philosophy. See J. Maritain, *Philosophy of Nature; The Degrees of Knowledge,* pp. 55, 56, 60-64, 136-201; *Science and Wisdom,* pp. 34-69.

[8] For the distinction between the two meanings of theology, see below, Q. 5, a. 4, pp. 52-53.

[9] See Aristotle, *Metaphysics* 6.1, 1026a18; 11.7, 1064b1-6.

bodies along with the bodies themselves in which they exist. Mathematics studies, apart from matter, forms of bodies that must exist in matter (e.g., lines, circles, numbers). Theology studies forms that are entirely separate from matter (e.g., God).[10]

It is clear from this that Boethius' division of the sciences, to some extent like that of Plato,[11] is based upon an objective division of reality. Each science has for its object a type of form more or less independent of matter. The branches of science exactly correspond to the order of forms themselves arranged in the real world according to their separation from matter. In such a view, there is little need to investigate the *subjective acts* by which the different objects of the sciences are grasped. The intellect follows more or less passively the division of forms it finds ready-made in the world. Only in the case of mathematics is there opportunity for discussing the act whereby the object of the science is attained, for, while existing in matter, mathematical forms are *considered* separate from matter. Yet Boethius does not exploit this opportunity, as St. Thomas does in his important third Article of Question Five.

In this Article St. Thomas shows the essential role played by the operations of the intellect in the determination of the subjects of the sciences.[12] The sciences are no longer considered as differentiated according to a distinction of forms ready-made in the world, but according to distinctions the mind itself makes in the course of its investigation of reality. Thus he changes the very notion of the object of a science. It is no longer a *form* in the Boethian sense, even

[10] See Boethius, *De Trinitate* 2, below, p. 3.

[11] See Plato, *Republic* 6.509-511.

[12] The pages that follow (xvi-xxi) are an analysis of this Article. The reader should also consult St. Thomas, *In I Phys.* lect. 1, n. 1-3; *In Meta.* Prooemium, trans. below, Appendix 2; *In I Meta.* lect. 10, n. 158, *III*, lect. 7, n. 405, *XI*, lect. 7, n. 2259-2267; *Summa Theol.* 1.40.3; 1.85.1, ad 1ᵐ, 2ᵐ.

though he sometimes uses the language of Boethius. Each science is said to have its own *subject* (*subjectum*), which differentiates that science from every other. By the subject of a science St. Thomas does not simply mean the things considered by the science, or its subject-matter. The term also designates the formal perspective (*ratio*) under which these things are considered in the science.[13]

The analogy that St. Thomas sees between a science and its subject and a faculty of the soul or a *habitus* and its object may help to clarify this point. He says, "The relation between a science and its subject is the same as that between a faculty or a *habitus* and its object. Now, properly speaking the object of a faculty or a *habitus* is that under whose formal perspective (*ratio*) all things are referred to that faculty or *habitus*; as man and stone are referred to sight in that they are colored. Hence 'colored thing' is the proper object of sight."[14] Completing this analogy, we can say that the subject of a science is that under whose formal perspective all things are studied in that science; as in metaphysics all things are considered from the point of view of being. Consequently, the subject of metaphysics is being according as it is being.

Once this viewpoint of the subject of science is adopted, it becomes imperative to study the operations of our intellect and the different distinctions it makes in considering reality. Now the human intellect, St. Thomas says, has basically two operations. The first is the understanding or apprehension of intelligible objects, by which we know more or less distinctly *what* things are, or in other words their essences. The second operation is judgment, by which we

[13] See below, Q. 5, a. 1, Reply to 6, p. 22. For the meaning of the subject of a science, see St. Thomas, *In I Post Anal.* lect. 2, n. 2-3, lect. 15, n. 3-4, lect. 25, n. 2; *In Meta.* Prooemium, trans. below, Appendix 2.

[14] *Summa Theol.* 1.1.7.

compose or divide what we have grasped in simple apprehension. For instance, having understood what green and grass are, we unite the two in affirming, "Grass is green"; or having grasped what man and stone are, we divide the two by denying, "Man is not a stone." In judgment, then, the intellect does not simply know *what* things are; rather, it grasps them in their very existence. For when we affirm that grass *is* green, we understand how grass exists, namely as green; and when we judge that man is not a stone, we understand how man does not exist, namely as a stone. That is why St. Thomas says that the first operation of the mind is directed to the essence of a being, whereas judgment is directed to its existence.[15]

Now, St. Thomas goes on to say, we can distinguish or abstract through both these operations of the intellect.[16] Abstraction through simple apprehension is the absolute consideration of some intelligible essence or nature; for instance, the consideration of animality in man without considering his rationality. This way of abstracting, connected as it is with simple apprehension, takes no account of the existence or non-existence of these objects of thought. It is simply concerned with them as distinct intelligible natures. The second way of abstracting, however, does take existence into account, for it is

---

[15] See below, Q. 5, a. 3, p. 35. See also *In I Sent.* 19, 5, I, ad 7^m; 38, 1, 3. Also J. Maritain, *Existence and the Existent*, pp. 10-19; E. Gilson, *Being and Some Philosophers*, pp. 190-215; G. B. Phelan, "Verum Sequitur Esse Rerum," *Mediaeval Studies* 1 (1939), 11-22.

[16] See below, Q. 5, a. 3, pp. 35-41. Also *Summa Theol.* 1.85.1, ad 1^m, 2^m. Abstraction has both a negative and positive aspect. It involves a detaching or separating, but primarily it is a positive concentration of the mind on some intelligible object or aspect of a thing without considering other objects or aspects of the same thing. "To abstract is not primarily to leave something out, but to take something in, and this is the reason why abstractions are knowledge." E. Gilson, *The Unity of Philosophical Experience*, pp. 144-145. See J. Maritain, *A Preface to Metaphysics*, p. 87.

accomplished through judgment. Thus if we judge, "Man is not a stone," we abstract or separate man from stone in such a way that we deny their identity, not simply as intelligible objects of thought, but in existence.

Once we grasp this distinction in the ways the intellect abstracts, it is not difficult to see that the laws of abstraction differ in the two cases. Obviously, the intellect cannot abstract or separate *in judgment* what is united in reality. This would be contrary to the truth, for in order that judgment be true, it must conform to the way things are. But if we judge, "The man is not white," separating in this way white from man, although in reality the man exists as white, then our judgment is false. As a consequence, we can only unite in our judgments what is united in existence, and separate or abstract in our judgments what is separate in existence.

This is not true, however, of abstraction through simple apprehension. In this operation of the intellect, we can, at least in some cases, abstract what is not separate in reality. As long as the intelligible object can be conceived apart, it can be considered by itself, even though it does not and cannot exist separately. For example, it is possible to consider human nature without considering the various individual men in whom that nature exists. For human nature is an intelligible object that can be conceived apart from individual men, although it cannot exist separately from them in reality.

In St. Thomas' view, the Platonic doctrine of separated Forms resulted from a confusion of these two modes of abstraction. Because the intellect can *consider* a nature or essence without thinking of the individuals whose nature it is, Plato thought that it must *exist* separate from them. So he confused the order of intelligibility and the order of existence. Because an object of thought is intelligible in itself, Plato thought that it must exist in itself. In fact, what is one in existence can be conceived in multiple fashion in simple apprehension. Only in negative judgment do we grasp the separation of one thing from another *in existence*. So the fact that we can consider a nature without considering the individuals in which it exists is no indication of the separate existence of that nature.

The immediate relevance, however, of the distinction between abstraction through apprehension and judgment goes beyond a refutation of Plato's theory of separate Forms. It enables us to distinguish between the subjects of natural philosophy and mathematics on the one hand, and that of metaphysics on the other. For according to St. Thomas the former grasp their subjects through abstraction in simple apprehension, while the latter attains its subject through a kind of abstraction accomplished in a negative judgment. In order to emphasize this difference he calls the latter sort of abstraction *separation*, reserving the term *abstraction* in the proper sense for that effected through simple apprehension.[17]

Let us now examine briefly the subjects of these sciences and the operations of the intellect whereby they are grasped.[18]

The abstraction of the natural philosopher is described as the abstraction of a whole: *abstractio totius*. By this is meant the absolute consideration of some essence without considering the individuals whose nature it is. The individuals are, as it were, "parts" from which the nature as a "whole" is abstracted. An abstraction of this sort is legitimate because these parts are accidental to the whole, in the sense that individuals as such are not contained in the definition of the nature. St. Thomas explains that all the sciences use this type of abstraction, for they all leave aside the individual and accidental features of their object of study and concentrate on those that belong

---

[17] See below, Q. 5, a. 3, pp. 40-41.
[18] See, *In Meta.* Prooemium, trans. below, Appendix 2; *In I Phys.* lect. 1, n. 1-3; *Summa Theol.* 1.85.1, ad 2ᵐ.

to it necessarily and universally. However, it is especially characteristic of natural philosophy, which studies the natures of material things. The natural philosopher cannot abstract from the essential "parts" of his subject-matter, namely those which necessarily belong to it and are included in its definition. He cannot, for example, leave out of consideration form or matter, for both are necessary parts of the nature of a material thing. He can, however, abstract from the individual as such, for this is not a necessary part of the nature. In studying man, for example, he cannot leave out of consideration flesh and bones, but he can abstract from *this* flesh and *these* bones.

The abstraction of the mathematician is an abstraction of form: *abstractio formae.* What is the meaning of "form" in this expression? It is not substantial form, for this cannot be conceived apart from matter, since it bears an essential relation to it: matter is included in the very definition of form. We can abstract a form from matter when its essence can be understood without matter, not, however, when its essence depends upon matter. For this reason we cannot abstract accidental form from substance, for an accident by definition is that whose nature it is to exist in a substance as in a subject. So it is impossible to abstract such a form from substance and understand it apart. Accidents, however, by nature inhere in substance in a definite order: quantity first, then quality, and only after that action and passion. So it is possible to conceive quantified substance without considering qualities, although the converse would be impossible. Consequently, the abstraction of form in mathematics is not an abstraction of the accidental form of quantity apart from substance. It does concern the form of quantity (at least if the mathematics in question is arithmetic or Euclidean geometry—the only types known to St. Thomas), but not apart from substance in which it inheres. Quantity is not abstracted from substance, but from the sensible qualities and the activities and passivities of material substance.[19]

The abstraction used by the metaphysician to grasp his subject is properly called separation: *separatio.* This is a radically different mode of abstraction from those we have already discussed, for it is effected through negative judgment, not through simple apprehension. We are thus forewarned that the subject of metaphysics will be radically different in character from those of natural philosophy and mathematics. For judgment is primarily pointed to the act of existing of things, whereas simple apprehension has to do rather with their essences or natures. As a result, the subject of metaphysics will have an existential character not found in those of the other two speculative sciences.[20]

Why, however, must the subject of metaphysics be grasped in a negative judgment? To understand this we must realize that for St. Thomas the subject of this science is universal being (*ens commune*), or being as being (*ens inquantum ens*). It also deals with the transcendental properties of being, such as goodness and truth, as well as with God, who is the first cause of universal being.[21] Now

---

[19] See below, Q. 5, a. 3, pp. 37-39. See also *Summa Theol.* 1.40.3; *In III Meta.* lect. 7, n. 405.

[20] This is also evident if we remember that for St. Thomas the act of existing (*esse*) is the supreme value of being, the actuality of all acts and the perfection of all perfections (*De Potentia* 7.2, ad 9^m). Hence metaphysics, which studies being from the point of view of being, or in other words from the point of view of that which is most perfect in being, is necessarily existential. See G. B. Phelan, "A Note on the Formal Object of Metaphysics," in *Essays in Modern Scholasticism*, pp. 47-51; R. J. Henle, *Method in Metaphysics*, pp. 51-58.

[21] See St. Thomas, *In Meta.* Prooemium, trans. below, Appendix 2; *In IV Meta.* lect. 1, n. 529-533. God is therefore not the subject of metaphysics, but the cause of its subject. He is not contained in being in general (*ens commune*), but transcends it. See St. Thomas, *Summa Theol.* 1.105.5; 1-2.66.5, ad 4^m. See also J.-D. Robert, "La métaphysique, science distincte de toute autre discipline philosophique selon

none of these depends on matter and motion for its existence, as do the objects of natural philosophy and mathematics. Some of them *can* exist in matter and motion, as for instance being, goodness, act and potency; but these can also be found apart from matter in spiritual beings. God, of course, exists absolutely independent of matter and movement. We can conclude, therefore, that the objects with which the metaphysician is concerned either actually exist or can exist without matter. And it is this truth that is grasped by him in a negative judgment in which he denies that being is necessarily bound up with matter and material conditions. Through a judgment of this sort he grasps being in its pure intelligibility, and primarily in its value of existence, and forms the metaphysical conception of being as being.[22]

---

saint Thomas d'Aquin," *Divus Thomas* 50 (1947), 206-222. God, however, is the principal object studied in metaphysics and the whole of that science is ordained to a knowledge of Him. (See below, Q. 5, a. 1, p. 14; *Contra Gentiles* 3.25.) That is why St. Thomas gives as its first name theology or divine science. (See *In Meta.* Proemium, trans. below, Appendix 2; Q. 5, a. 1, p. 14.) On the other hand, the theology of Sacred Scripture has God for its subject (see below, Q. 5, a. 4, p. 52).

There is no distinction for St. Thomas between a general metaphysics or ontology and philosophical theology. The theology of the philosophers and the primary philosophy or metaphysics are one and the same science. See J. Owens, "Theodicy, Natural Theology, and Metaphysics," *Modern Schoolman* 28 (1951), 126-137.

Consequently, we cannot accept the suggestion of Philip Merlan that, for St. Thomas, abstraction is the method by which general metaphysics treats of the transcendentals and separation is the method by which special metaphysics treats of immaterial substances. Neither this division of metaphysics nor this distinction between abstraction and separation is to be found in his works. See P. Merlan, "Abstraction and Metaphysics in St. Thomas' *Summa*," *Journal of the History of Ideas* 14 (1953), 284-291.

[22] As stated above (note 16), every abstraction has a positive as well as a negative aspect. This is true of abstraction through judgment as well as through simple apprehension. It would seem that the negative judgment of the metaphysician implies an affirmative judgment in which being, and particularly the act of

From this it should be clear that St. Thomas never envisaged one type of abstraction common to all the sciences which admits simply of three *degrees*. As Jacques Maritain has said, each of the speculative sciences attains its subject by a mode of abstraction that is *sui generis* and irreducible to any other. One does not simply continue the others along the same line, as if mathematical abstraction lays hold of a subject simply more abstract and general than that of natural philosophy, and metaphysical separation lays hold of one simply more abstract and general than that of mathematics. In other words, the term "abstraction" does not have a univocal meaning. It is analogical, signifying activities of the intellect which are essentially diverse from each other, although proportionately the same. Each of the modes of abstraction is a distinct type of "eidetic visualisation"—to use an expression of J. Maritain—a distinct way in which the intellect lays hold of reality. At the same time, each implies a distinct way of distinguishing one thing from another, or one aspect of a being from another aspect of the same being.[23] The difference

existing, are grasped in their positive value. For the role of separation in metaphysics, see J. Maritain, *Existence and the Existent*, p. 30, note; L.-B. Geiger, "Abstraction et séparation d'après s. Thomas," *Revue des sciences phil. et théol.* 31 (1947), 24-28; R. Schmidt, "L'emploi de la séparation en métaphysique," *Revue philosophique de Louvain* 58 (1960), 373-393; L. Sweeney, *A Metaphysics of Authentic Existentialism*, pp. 307-329, 345-346; J. Owens, "Metaphysical Separation in Aquinas," *Mediaeval Studies* 34 (1972), 287-306 (bibliography, p. 302, n. 39); L. Elders, *Faith and Science*, pp. 105-111; J. F. Wippel, *Metaphysical Themes in Thomas Aquinas*, ch. IV: Metaphysics and *Separatio* in Thomas Aquinas, pp. 69-104 (bibliography, p. 70, n. 3).

[23] Although J. Maritain uses the expression "degrees of abstraction," he warns us that there is not simply a difference of degree between these activities of the intellect. See *Philosophy of Nature*, p. 24; also *Existence and the Existent*, pp. 28-30. On this question, see the prudent remark of L.-M. Régis in "Un livre... La philosophie de la nature. Quelques apories," in *Études et Recherches. Philosophie* 1 (1936), 141, note 3. See also R. Allers, "On Intellectual Operations," *The New*

between the mode of abstraction pertaining to metaphysics on the one hand, and those pertaining to mathematics and natural philosophy on the other, is especially marked, for the former is accomplished through negative judgment, whereas the latter are the work of simple apprehension. It is this difference to which St. Thomas wishes to draw our attention when, in the present work, he calls the former *separation* and the latter *abstraction*. Both of these are said to be ways in which the intellect *distinguishes*, so that distinction appears as a quasi-genus of which separation and abstraction are diverse modes.[24]

It is true that in his later writings St. Thomas does not adhere to this terminology. For example, in his *Summa Theologiae* he speaks of two modes of *abstraction*, one through judgment, the other through apprehension. The term "separation" does not appear.[25] But this is not surprising, since even in his Commentary on the *De Trinitate* he uses the verb "to abstract" to designate the act of "separating."[26] St. Thomas sometimes uses terms in a wide sense and not with their precise meaning. But despite this difference of terminology there is no indication that he abandoned the views expressed in his early work—views that are so closely in accord with his fundamental philosophical principles.

It would be erroneous, however, to see no importance whatsoever in his effort at precision in terminology in his Commentary on the *De Trinitate*. As he himself says, words are signs of concepts; and a philosopher's struggle to make his vocabulary more precise can

---

Scholasticism 2 (1952), 25-26. The term "degree of abstraction" (*gradus abstractionis*) seems to have been first used by Robert Kilwardby (d. 1279) in his *De Ortu Scientiarum*, c. 25, p. 78, n. 203; c. 33, p. 119, n. 335.

[24] See below, p. 41.
[25] See St. Thomas, *Summa Theol.* 1.85.1, ad 1ᵐ, 2ᵐ.
[26] See below, Q. 5, a. 3, pp. 35-36.

generally be taken as an indication that he is doing the same with his thoughts.

That this is true in the present case is evident from St. Thomas' autograph manuscript of his Commentary on the *De Trinitate*. A study of the manuscript reveals that he began the Reply to Question Five, Article Three, several times, and that the final redaction was achieved only after great effort at precision of thought and terminology.[27]

In the first redaction St. Thomas makes no mention of the distinction between apprehension and judgment: the distinction that later becomes the keystone of his solution. His thought moves entirely in the order of essence or quiddity and the various ways in which the intellect becomes assimilated to it. A threefold division is attempted on the basis of the simultaneity, anteriority and posteriority of essences and their various elements, and again on the basis of their dependence on, or independence of each other. But no conclusion is reached along these lines, and he takes up the question again in a second redaction. Here at once he introduces the fundamental distinction between apprehension and judgment, but it still does not play the important role assigned to it in the definitive redaction. He speaks of "modes of abstraction" instead of "modes of distinguishing" as in the final writing; and the explanation of the three modes tends as before to remain on the level of simple apprehension, essences and their elements, their simultaneity, anteriority and posteriority. Only in the final redaction does he bring out the crucial importance of judgment and the act of existing (*esse*) grasped in that act. Only here does he establish the basic difference

---

[27] See the study of these redactions by L.-B. Geiger, "Abstraction." They have been edited by P. A. Uccelli, *S. Thomae Aquinatis in Boetium de Trinitate Expositio* (Rome, 1880), pp. 335-337; also by B. Decker, *Expositio super Librum Boethii De Trinitate* (Leiden, 1955), pp. 230-234.

between the intellectual operations by which the metaphysician lays hold of his subject and those by which the natural philosopher and mathematician lay hold of theirs.

The direction in which St. Thomas' mind was moving in these various redactions is clear. He was progressively realizing the central role of judgment and existence in the solution of his problem, as well as the eminently existential character of the subject of metaphysics.

In recent years historians of St. Thomas' philosophy have become more fully conscious of these aspects of his thought which for a long time remained quite obscured and forgotten.[28] Indeed two of his outstanding followers in the sixteenth and seventeenth centuries, Cajetan and John of St. Thomas, taught a doctrine of abstraction and division of the sciences based on it which leaves out of consideration the very features St. Thomas took such pains to emphasize: the role of judgment and existence. They distinguish between "total abstraction" and "formal abstraction." What is abstracted in the former is as a universal whole with respect to that from which it is abstracted; what is abstracted in the latter is as a form of that from which it is abstracted. All the sciences, they add, use total abstraction, but they are diversified according to modes of formal abstraction.[29]

It is beyond the scope of this Introduction to attempt an adequate study of their doctrine and an evaluation of it as a faithful continuation of St. Thomas'. But this at least should be pointed out: for

---

[28] Among other works, see E. Gilson, *The Christian Philosophy of St. Thomas Aquinas*; *Elements of Christian Philosophy*; *Being and Some Philosophers*. J. Maritain, *A Preface to Metaphysics*; *Existence and the Existent*. J. de Finance, *Être et agir dans la philosophie de s. Thomas*. G. B. Phelan, "Being and the Metaphysicians," in *From an Abundant Spring*, pp. 423-447.

[29] See Cajetan, *In De Ente et Essentia*, Prooemium, Q. 1, n. 5, pp. 6, 7; *De Nominum Analogia* 5, p. 50; John of St. Thomas, *Ars Logica* 2, Q. 27, a. 1, pp. 818-830.

St. Thomas,, abstraction of a whole, although common to all the sciences, is especially characteristic of natural philosophy, whereas for Cajetan and John of St. Thomas, total abstraction is used by all the sciences but properly defines none of them. Again, for St. Thomas abstraction of form is proper to mathematics, while for his two commentators formal abstraction belongs to all the sciences, which are diversified by its various modes.[30] Finally, and most important of all, these commentators fail to explain the essential role negative judgment plays in St. Thomas' metaphysics, and the existential character of its subject. There are grounds to suspect, therefore, that behind the difference in the terminology of St. Thomas and his commentators there is a difference of doctrine.[31] This much at

[30] The terms themselves ("formal abstraction," "total abstraction") are not equivalent to St. Thomas' "abstraction of a form" and "abstraction of a whole." *Formal* and *total* qualify the act of abstraction; *of a form* and *of a whole* designate the object of the abstraction.

[31] See L.-M. Régis, "Un livre," pp. 138-140. The opposite view is expressed by J. Maritain, *Existence and the Existent*, p. 30, note; also by M.-V. Leroy, "Le Savoir spéculatif," in *Jacques Maritain, son œuvre philosophique*, pp. 236-339, and "Abstractio et separatio d'après un texte controversé de Saint Thomas (*In Lib. Boeth. de Trin.*, V, 3 & 4)," *Revue Thomiste* 48 (1948), 328-339. J. Maritain has replied to Fr. Régis in *Quatre Essais sur l'esprit dans sa condition charnelle* (Paris, 1956), p. 216, n. 21.

Among the many articles on the subject are: F. G. Connolly, "Science vs. Philosophy," *The Modern Schoolman* 29 (1952), 197-209, and "Abstraction and Moderate Realism," *The New Scholasticism* 27 (1953), 72-90; V. Smith, "Abstraction and the Empiriological Method," *Proceedings of the American Catholic Philosophical Association*, 1952, pp. 35-50; G. Van Riet, "La théorie thomiste de l'abstraction," *Revue philosophique de Louvain* 50 (1952), 353-393; P. Merlan, "Abstraction and Metaphysics in St. Thomas' *Summa*," *Journal of the History of Ideas* 14 (1953), 284-291; W. Kane, "Abstraction and the Distinction of the Sciences," *The Thomist* 17 (1954), 43-68; E. Simmons, "In Defense of Total and Formal Abstraction," *The New Scholasticism* 29 (1955), 427-440, and "The Thomistic Doctrine of the Three Degrees of Formal Abstraction," *The Thomist* 22 (1959), 37-67; F. Cunningham, "A Theory on Abstraction in St. Thomas," *The Modern Schoolman* 35 (1958), 249-270.

least is certain: without a direct contact with the works of St.
Thomas, especially with his Commentary on the *De Trinitate*, it is
impossible to appreciate his authentic teaching.

St. Thomas' conception of abstraction and the hierarchy of the
sciences owes much to Aristotle. Yet it should be pointed out that
he adds notions of his own and that even the ones he borrows from
the Greek philosopher generally take on a quite original meaning in
the context of his philosophy. This is not the place to attempt an
adequate comparison of Aristotle's doctrine with that of St. Thomas.
Aristotle's views on these subjects are extremely difficult to understand and no brief account could do them justice. However, it may
be helpful to the reader to say a few words on this topic. Some
suggested readings will help him to carry on the study for himself.[32]

It should be remarked, first of all, that when Aristotle uses the
term "abstraction" in connection with the sciences, it does not have
the analogical character it has for St. Thomas. There is no doctrine
of "degrees" of abstraction in Aristotle's philosophy of the sciences.[33] For him, abstraction in the technical sense means the act by
which mathematical entities are grasped; namely those that are not
separate from sensible things, but that are considered by the
mathematician as separate. The mathematician subtracts and leaves
out of consideration sensible forms, retaining only quantity.[34] The
natural philosopher, on the other hand, attains his object by addition; for in his science forms are grasped, not as separated, but as
immanent in the matter that they determine. Hence they must be

---

[32] See M.-D. Philippe, "Abstraction, addition, séparation dans la philosophie
d'Aristote," *Revue Thomiste* 48 (1948), 461-479; J. Owens, *The Doctrine of Being
in the Aristotelian Metaphysics*, pp. 381-385.

[33] See J. Owens, *Doctrine of Being*, p. 385.

[34] See M.-D. Philippe, "Abstraction," pp. 461-466; J. Owens, *Doctrine*,
pp. 382-383.

understood with the addition of matter, which enters into the definition of the objects of this science.[35]

To appreciate the import of addition in Aristotle's philosophy, we must realize that for him the form or essence of a material thing does not include matter. Only the concrete entity does.[36] And since it is this concrete entity or substance that is defined by the natural philosopher, an act of addition is required to grasp form and matter together. St. Thomas, however, does not require such an operation, for according to him the essence of a material thing at once includes both form and matter.[37]

Aristotle is not so explicit in designating the intellectual activity characteristic of primary philosophy or metaphysics. However, he does describe it as an act of contemplation; and this act would seem to imply a separation, for its object is either separated in reality from the material world, like the separated substances, or it is at least capable of being separated in thought, like being, act, potency, etc.[38]

---

[35] See M.-D. Philippe, "Abstraction," pp. 466-469; J. Owens, *Doctrine of Being*, p. 384.

[36] See Aristotle, *Metaphysics* 7.7, 1032b1-2, b14; 7.10, 1035a17-22; 7.11, 1037a25-29. See also J. Owens, *Doctrine of Being*, pp. 360-364.

[37] See below, Q. 5, a. 2, p. 27 and note 16. St. Thomas refers to addition when commenting on Aristotle (see *In III De Caelo et Mundo*, lect. 3, n. 4). It finds no place, however, in his personal doctrine.

St. Thomas' conception of essence is not identical with that of Aristotle. The mediaeval Arabian philosopher Averroes followed Aristotle's notion of essence as form without matter (see Averroes, *In VII Meta.*, t. c. 21, fol. 171I; t. c. 34, fol. 184D). St. Thomas criticizes Averroes for teaching that the whole essence of a species is the form alone without matter, but he does not recognize this doctrine as Aristotelian. Rather, he benignly interprets Aristotle's doctrine as in accord with his own. See St. Thomas, *In VII Meta.* lect. 9, n. 1467-1469. See also A. Maurer, "Form and Essence in the Philosophy of St. Thomas," *Mediaeval Studies* 13 (1951), 165-176.

[38] See M.-D. Philippe, "Abstraction," pp. 469-479; J. Owens, *Doctrine of Being*, pp. 384-385.

Nothing explicit is said, however, about these objects being attained through a negative judgment of separation; and they lack the existential character that they have in St. Thomas' metaphysics.

These observations should put us on our guard against speaking without qualification of an "Aristotelico-Thomistic" doctrine of abstraction and scheme of the sciences. Although St. Thomas owes much to Aristotle on these points, to link together in this way the views of the two philosophers is a simplification that loses sight of important divergences in doctrine.[39]

*
* *

We come now to the main theme of Question Six: the special methods of the speculative sciences. This will give us a new criterion for distinguishing these sciences: they not only have distinct subjects of inquiry; they also have their own characteristic methods of procedure in harmony with their subjects.

It will be noticed at once that St. Thomas adopts a pluralist attitude toward scientific method; he does not propose one method for all sciences. He recognizes, of course, that they have a common method in that they follow the same basic laws of logic;[40] but besides this he maintains that each science has its own special way of inquiring after truth. Because scientific methods are not equal in the certitude they yield, there will always be a temptation to deny this and to extend one method to all the sciences because of its excellence. St. Thomas saw that there is a particular temptation to single out the mathematical method for this role, since it is the most exact

[39] See the remarks of L.-M. Régis, "Un livre," pp. 128-138.
[40] See St. Thomas, *In II Meta.* lect. 5, n. 335; also below, Q. 5, a. 1, Reply to 2 and 3, pp. 16-17; Q. 6, a. 1, Reply to 3, pp. 69-70.

and certain. But he warns against this, insisting on the specificity of method in each of the sciences.[41]

The physico-mathematical sciences are no exception to this rule. Although they were merely in their infancy in the thirteenth century, St. Thomas recognized their epistemological type and describes it with a greater acumen than anyone else in his day. He calls them "intermediate sciences" because they are located between natural science and mathematics and thus share the characteristics of both. He names astronomy, optics, and harmony or music as examples. Sciences of this sort study the physical universe, but by means of mathematics. So mathematics plays a formal role in their structure, while physical reality plays a material role.[42] But even though the rule of analysis and deduction in these sciences is mathematical, their method is not simply that of mathematics. Since they are physical sciences on their material side, they must be fed through a contact of the senses with material things. As a result, they have a method distinct from that of natural science and mathematics, although it shares to some extent in the methods of both.

In describing the methods of the main branches of the sciences St. Thomas adopts the classical terminology of Boethius. The philosophy of nature, he says, proceeds *rationabiliter*, mathematics *disciplinabiliter*, and metaphysics *intellectualiter*.[43] For want of better

---

[41] See *In II Meta.* lect. 5, n. 335-337; also below, Q. 6, a. 2, p. 79: "... they are in error who try to proceed in the same way in these three parts of speculative science." Here St. Thomas opposes the notion, which has become prevalent in our day, that science is essentially one, with the same scientific method. Descartes did much to introduce this conception into modern thought. See J. Maritain, *The Dream of Descartes*, pp. 48-57; also E. Gilson, *The Unity of Philosophical Experience*, pp. 142-151. The latter is an historical study of what happened to philosophy when methods other than its own were applied to it.

[42] See below, Q. 5, a. 3, Reply to 5, 6 and 7, pp. 43-45, and note 22.

[43] See below, Q. 6, a. 1, p. 58, and note 2.

terms, these Latin words have been translated respectively: "according to the mode of reason" or "rationally," "according to the mode of learning," and "according to the mode of intellect" or "intellectually." Some explanation of these terms is required.

The terms "reason" and "intellect," with which the methods of the philosophy of nature and metaphysics are respectively related, are almost synonyms, although we associate reason more particularly with the power of drawing conclusions from principles and intellect with the power of simply knowing or understanding. For St. Thomas, reason and intellect are not really distinct powers of man. They are one and the same intellectual power by which we know in different ways. Through reason we move from the known to the unknown, advancing from one thing to another in our conquest of truth. Through intellect we grasp an intelligible truth simply and intuitively, without any movement or discourse of the mind. So the act of reason is compared to that of intellect as movement to rest, or as the reaching out for something to the actual possession of it. Again, they are compared as the imperfect to the perfect, as a circle to its centre, as time to eternity.[44]

Reasoning is especially characteristic of man, for he must acquire knowledge through inquiry and discovery. That is why he is properly a *rational* animal. But he also knows by understanding. Indeed every movement of his reason begins and ends in understanding, just as every step we take in walking begins and ends at a position of rest. And just as every step we take brings us closer to our goal, so the movement of reason leads to a deeper understanding of truth, which is the object of our intellect.

It is quite different with the angels. They do not have to reason. Intellectual beings by nature, they grasp intuitively a multitude of

---

[44] See St. Thomas, *Summa Theol.* 1.79.8.

truths in the unity of a single idea.[45] In this respect they resemble God, who simply by knowing his essence knows all things. Human reason, on the other hand, as the most imperfect of all intellects, must grasp unity in multiplicity rather than multiplicity in unity. Human knowledge begins in the senses, which present reason with a vast variety of data; but in this multiplicity it sees unity and thus gathers simple truths from it. At the end of its reasoning, therefore, the human mind approaches the angelic intellect in gathering up a multitude of truths in the unity of simple principles or ideas. St. Thomas says: "... it is distinctive of reason to disperse itself in the consideration of many things and then to gather one simple truth from them." And he quotes with approval the words of Dionysius the pseudo-Areopagite: "Souls have the power of reasoning in that they approach the truth of things from various angles, and in this respect they are inferior to angels; but inasmuch as they gather a multiplicity into unity they are in a way equal to the angels."[46]

It is against the background of this distinction of reason and intellect that we must understand St. Thomas' views on the methods of the sciences. Natural philosophy, he tells us, uses a method most in harmony with our natural way of knowing as rational beings.[47] For this reason its method is properly called *rational*. To begin with, this science deals with the changing sensible world, which is our first and most congenial object of knowledge, the one that our reason is best adapted to understand. It stays closest to this world in its changing and sensible character, and in the multiplicity of data it presents to us. Hence the very method it uses is characterized by the analysis of manifold data and by movement and progression from one thing to another. Then too, as rational beings, all of whose knowledge

---

[45] See St. Thomas, ibid., 1.58.3.
[46] See below, Q. 6, a. 1, Reply to the Third Question, p. 71.
[47] See below, Q. 6, a. 1, Reply to the First Question, pp. 65-66.

originates in the senses, we must investigate the properties of things and their sensible appearances in order to know their natures. We must inquire into effects in order to discover their causes. This movement of reason from effect to cause, from sign to thing signified, is particularly characteristic of natural philosophy and most connatural to us as rational animals. What is more, unlike mathematics, natural philosophy does not move simply from one object of thought to another logically distinct object of thought. It is concerned with existing changing beings in their diversity and interrelations. In other words, it not only demonstrates by way of formal causes, but also through efficient and final causes, one of which is entirely external to the other. On this score, too, it uses a method that is rational in the proper sense of the word, for it follows most closely the human reason's natural way of knowing.

St. Thomas also attributes a major role to reasoning in mathematics.[48] In this respect it is like natural philosophy. The difference in their methods lies in the causes employed in reasoning. Mathematical demonstrations begin with definitions and principles, from which conclusions are deduced by way of formal causality. For example, a certain property of the triangle is shown to follow from its very definition. Unlike natural philosophy, mathematics does not demonstrate through final or efficient causes.

Following Boethius and a long-established tradition, St. Thomas says that mathematics proceeds "according to the mode of learning" (*disciplinabiliter*). This does not describe the mathematical method intrinsically, as "rational" describes that of natural philosophy. It simply designates that the mathematical sciences are the easiest to learn, for they are most exact and certain. The antiquity of this

---

[48] See below, Q. 6, a. 1, Reply to the First Question, pp. 65-66; Reply to argument 4 of Second Question, p. 70.

notion is indicated by the very etymology of the word "mathe-
matics." It comes from the Greek *mathein* which means "to learn."
Its equivalent in Latin is *discere*, from which *disciplina* and the
English "discipline" are derived.

St. Thomas always maintained that we achieve our greatest
certitude in mathematics.[49] It is more certain than natural philosophy
because it abstracts from motion and the sensible qualities of
material things. Natural philosophy must take all of these into
account, and so it is more difficult and less certain. The demonstrations of this science often hold good only in the majority of cases:
there are exceptions because of the contingency of matter.

Furthermore, although natural philosophy studies material things,
we do not know their substantial essences in themselves. Whatever
knowledge we can have of them is attained through their accidental
characteristics—their quantity, qualities, operations, etc.—which are
signs of their essential properties. In other words, the natural
philosopher knows his objects of study very imperfectly through
their sensible appearances.[50] This is why St. Thomas qualifies so
strictly the type of certitude we can expect in natural science. He
does not deny that some of its reasonings furnish adequate proof and
are true demonstrations; but others are simply "suppositions,"

---

[49] See below, Q. 6, a. 1, Reply to the Second Question, p. 67; also *In II Meta.*
lect. 5, n. 336. From the point of view of the simplicity of its objects, metaphysics
is the most certain science (see *In I Meta.* lect. 2, n. 47). It is not the most certain
science, however, with reference to us, or subjectively, owing to the weakness of our
intellects. For the different meanings of certitude, see St. Thomas, *Summa Theol.*
2-2.4.8.

[50] See St. Thomas, *De Ente et Essentia* 5, ed. Leonine, p. 379.76-80; Eng. trans.
p. 64, n. 6. See also *De Spiritualibus Creaturis* 11, ad 3^m, Eng. trans. p. 132;
Summa Theol. 1.29.1, ad 3^m; 1.77.1, ad 7^m; *In I De Anima,* lect. 1, n. 15, Eng.
trans. pp. 49-50; *Contra Gentiles* 1.3. See J. Maritain, *The Degrees of Knowledge,*
pp. 176-178, 206-209.

which explain sensible appearances without being necessarily true. For example, St. Thomas considers that although the Ptolemaic system of astronomy "saves the appearances," it is not necessarily true, since the appearances of the stars might conceivably be "saved" in still another way not yet known to man.[51]

The mathematical method is also more certain than that of metaphysics, but for another reason. The objects of metaphysics, like God, the angels, being, goodness, truth, are too lofty for the human reason. They can be known only with the greatest difficulty and hence with a lesser degree of certitude than mathematical entities. However, there is this consolation for the metaphysician: the little he can know about these most lofty matters is of greater value than the vast amount that can be known about those that are mundane.[52]

Indeed, in the realm of metaphysics the human intellect is strained to its utmost and is forced to adopt a method little congenial to it: the method of intellectual insight. For in this science it deals with objects, some of which transcend itself, and all of which are purely intelligible and as such do not fall under the senses or the imagination. In knowing these objects it must use a method that is not *rational*, but rather resembles that of the angelic intelligences. The method of metaphysics, St. Thomas says, is properly *intellectual* because it stays closest to the mode of knowing characteristic of intellect, as the method of natural philosophy is properly rational because it stays closest to the mode of knowing proper to reason.[53] By this he does not mean that metaphysics makes no use of reasoning, or that natural philosophy makes no use of intellectual

---

[51] See St. Thomas, *In I De Caelo et Mundo*, lect. 3, n. 7; *II*, lect. 17, n. 2; *Summa Theol.* 1.32.1, ad 2m.

[52] See St. Thomas, *Expositio super Librum de Causis*, lect. 1; trans. below, Appendix 3.

[53] See below, Q. 6, a. 1, Reply to the Third Question, p. 70.

insight. It is simply a question of greater emphasis on one or the other phase of human knowledge. In natural philosophy the movement of reason predominates, in metaphysics the unwavering grasp of fundamental truths through simple insight or intuition.[54] If metaphysics uses discursive reasoning, and moves from principles to conclusions, its conclusions are closest to its principles and so its reasoning most closely resembles intellectual intuition. Its method is accordingly more simple and less complicated than that of either natural philosophy or mathematics. It is a method of synthesis rather than analysis,[55] for it is not so much a gleaning of simple truths from a multitude of data, as seeing a multitude of truths in the unity of simple truths. For metaphysics comes at the end of man's natural knowledge as its crown and completion, just as intellectual insight comes at the end of reasoning. The analytic movement of reason in all the sciences finds its ultimate term in the intellectual insights of metaphysics, whether the object under consideration is God as the first cause of all things, or being and the properties of being as being as the most universal of all conceptions.[56]

[54] As a consequence, natural philosophy progresses in a different way from metaphysics. Movement from one thing to another and change of doctrine are more accentuated in natural philosophy than in metaphysics, which develops rather by penetrating more and more deeply into the same truths which are ever ancient and ever new. J. Maritain remarks that a treatise on natural philosophy can at the most endure a lifetime, and even then it must be periodically revised to take into account new data. This is not true of metaphysics, whose rhythm of development is different because of its greater independence of the natural sciences. On the other hand, science in the modern sense moves and changes in its theories with a greater rapidity than natural philosophy. The distinction between the methods and development of natural philosophy and metaphysics is verified proportionately between philosophy as a whole and science in the modern sense of the word. See J. Maritain, *Science and Wisdom*, p. 64; *A Preface to Metaphysics*, pp. 2-16.

[55] In the sense in which these terms are defined below, Q. 6, a. 1, Reply to the Third Question, p. 71.

[56] See below, Q. 6, a. 1, Reply to the Third Question, p. 72.

St. Thomas throws further light on the methods of the speculative sciences in Article Two of Question Six. The specific problem raised there is whether metaphysics must in any way use the imagination; but the solution involves the more general problem of the relation of the sciences to the senses, imagination, and intellect.

In resolving this problem, he points out first that all our knowledge begins in the senses. So the starting-point of all the sciences must be the same: they must all originate in the senses. Our knowledge, however, ends in an intellectual judgment, and this judgment is made in different ways in the different sciences. In natural philosophy the judgment "terminates" in the senses. By this St. Thomas means that the judgment is made in the light of what the senses reveal: their evidence is the final court of appeal for the veracity of the scientific judgment. In mathematics the judgment "terminates" in the imagination, in the sense that the mathematical judgment looks to the evidence presented by the imagination. When he says this, St. Thomas is thinking of such mathematical sciences as Euclidean geometry, in which the mathematical entities are directly imaginable, and the judgment of the mathematician is directly verified by an appeal to the imagination. The problem of non-Euclidean geometries, in which a direct appeal to the imagination is impossible, did not arise in his day.[57] Finally, the judgment of the metaphysician "terminates" in the intellect alone. It could not possibly terminate in the senses or the imagination, for these faculties grasp things under their qualitative and quantitative aspects, whereas the objects of metaphysics are separated from matter and material conditions both in existence and in thought. Its objects are

---

[57] The conclusions of non-Euclidean geometries are only indirectly verifiable in the intuition of the imagination. See J. Maritain, *The Degrees of Knowledge*, pp. 53-55, 165-167.

purely intelligible, and it is only the intellect that apprehends things under this aspect. Of course the metaphysician must use his senses and imagination as the source of his knowledge, but he makes his judgments in the light of what the intellect reveals about things, not according as they are grasped by the lower faculties of the soul. This final observation gives us a new criterion for distinguishing the speculative sciences from each other, and it offers new evidence that it would be a mistake to think that they must all use the same method.

In broad outline this is the picture of the hierarchy of the speculative sciences and of their methods drawn by St. Thomas in the present work. We leave the reader to fill out the many details by a careful reading of the text, including the illuminating answers to objections. Abundant notes are appended to direct him to other writings of the Angelic Doctor for additional clarification of his doctrines. Reference is also made wherever possible to works on St. Thomas' philosophy which throw light on the more difficult passages. With their assistance it is hoped that the modern reader will be able to make contact with his thought and share in its order and wisdom.

*
* *

The translation was made from Bruno Decker's edition of St. Thomas' Commentary, published in 1955 and slightly corrected in the reprint of 1959.[58] P.-M. Gils made further suggestions for

---

[58] *Expositio super librum Boethii De Trinitate*, ed. Bruno Decker (Leiden: Brill, 1955; reprint with corrections 1959). For these corrections, see B. Decker, "Corrigenda et Addenda à l'édition du 'In Boethium de Trinitate' de S. Thomas d'Aquin," *Scriptorium* 13 (1959), 81-82.

improving the Latin text, some of which I have adopted in the translation.[59]

The previous editions of the translation did not include a translation of the opening lines of Boethius' *De Trinitate*, chapter 2, or St. Thomas' literal commentary on them. These have been included in the present edition as an introduction to the Questions.

A translation of Questions I-IV of St. Thomas' Commentary has been prepared and it will be published in a separate volume. This will complete the translation of the Commentary.

The place and date of publication of works cited in the notes are given in the bibliography.

---

[59] P.-M. Gils, *Bulletin Thomiste* 11 (1960-1961), no. 54, pp. 41-44.

Thomas Aquinas

Commentary on the
De Trinitate
of Boethius,
Questions v-vi

Boethius
De Trinitate, Chapter 2

Therefore, come, let us delve in and examine each subject as far as it can be grasped and understood; for as has been wisely said,[1] in my opinion, it is a scholar's duty to try to formulate his opinion about each thing as it actually is.

There are three divisions of speculative science:

Natural science deals with motion and is not abstract (ἀνυπεξαίρε-τος), for it is concerned with the forms of bodies along with matter, which forms cannot be separated in reality from their bodies. These bodies are in motion (earth, for example, tending downward and fire tending upward), and the form that is joined[2] with the matter takes on its movement.

Mathematics does not deal with motion and it is not abstract, for it inquires into the forms of bodies apart from matter and therefore apart from motion, which forms, however, since they exist in matter, cannot be separated from bodies.

Theology does not deal with motion and it is abstract and separable, for the divine substance is without either matter or motion.

In the natural sciences, then, we shall have to follow the mode of reasoning in our thinking, in mathematics the mode of learning, and

---

[1] Perhaps Cicero. See his *Tusculan Disputations*, 5, c. 7, n. 19; ed. King, p. 444.23-25.

[2] Reading *coniuncta* with the edition of Stewart-Rand-Tester, p. 8.10, and St. Thomas' commentary, ed. Decker, p. 159.16.

in divine science the mode of intellection; and in divine science we should not be turned aside to images but rather apprehend form itself, [which is truly form and no image, which is being itself and the source of being].

St. Thomas' Literal Commentary

Boethius previously[3] set forth the teaching of the Catholic faith about the unity of the Trinity and he investigated the meaning of that doctrine. Now he intends to begin to inquire into his previous statements. And because, in the Philosopher's opinion,[4] we must investigate the method of a science before the science itself, he divides this section into two parts. First Boethius explains the method suited to this inquiry, which concerns divine things. Second, at the words "which is truly form," etc., using the assigned method he proceeds to investigate the proposed subject. The first part has two divisions. In the first he states the necessity of explaining the method of inquiry. In the second, which begins "There are three," etc., he shows the method appropriate to the present inquiry.

He says "Therefore," making it clear that this is the teaching of the Catholic faith concerning the unity of the Trinity, and that absence of difference is the reason for the unity, "come" (an adverb of exhortation), "let us delve in," that is, let us make an intimate inquiry, closely investigating the deepest principles of things and thoroughly examining the truth, which is as it were veiled and hidden, and we should do so in an appropriate manner. So he adds, "and examine each subject" under discussion "as far as it can be grasped and understood," that is, in the way in which it can be grasped and understood.

---

[3] See Boethius, *De Trinitate*, c. 1; ed. Stewart-Rand-Tester, pp. 7-9.

[4] Aristotle, *Metaphysics* 2.3, 995a13.

He uses these two words ["grasped" and "understood"] because the method of investigating anything should conform both to things and to us. If it did not conform to things, they could not be understood, if it did not conform to us, we could not grasp them, since divine things are of such a nature that they can only be known by the intellect. If we wanted to follow the imagination in investigating them, we could not understand, because the realities themselves are not intelligible in this way. If we wanted to see divine things in themselves and to comprehend them with the same certitude as sensible things and mathematical proofs are comprehended, this sort of apprehension would elude us because of the weakness of our intellect, even though the realities themselves are in their own right intelligible in this way. That a suitable method should be observed in every inquiry he proves by appealing to the authority of the Philosopher, adding "for as has been wisely said, in my opinion," namely by Aristotle in the beginning of the *Ethics*,[5] "it is a scholar's duty to try to formulate his opinion about each thing as it actually is," that is, in a manner adapted to the thing itself. For equal certainty and demonstrative evidence cannot be provided for everything. The words of the Philosopher in the first book of the *Ethics* are: "For it is the mark of an educated man to look for as much certitude in each class of things as the nature of the subject admits."[6]

When he says, "There are three," etc., he examines the method suited to this inquiry [of theology], distinguishing it from the methods employed in the other sciences. Because the method should

[5] This statement is not found literally in Aristotle's *Ethics*. It was ascribed by some earlier medieval writers, to whom the *Ethics* was unknown, to Cicero. See, for example, Gilbert of Poitiers, *Expositio in Boecii librum primum de Trinitate*; PL 64: 1265B; ed. N. Häring, p. 79.36. For the reference to Cicero, see above, note 1.

[6] Aristotle, *Nicomachean Ethics* 1.1, 1094b23-25.

be suited to the matter under investigation, this part has two divisions. First, he distinguishes the sciences according to the things they deal with; second, at the words "In the natural sciences," etc., he indicates the methods suited to each of them.

Regarding the first, he makes three points. First, he indicates the objects studied by natural philosophy; second, those studied by mathematics, when he says "Mathematics," etc.; third, those studied by divine science, when he says "Theology does not deal with motion," etc. He asserts, then, that it has been well said that one ought to formulate his belief about anything in the way it actually is. "There are three divisions of speculative science," or philosophy (he says this to differentiate it from ethics, which is active or practical), and in all three there is needed a method suited to the subject matter. The three divisions mentioned above are physics or natural science, mathematics and divine science or theology.[7] Since, I say, there are three divisions, "Natural science," which is one of them, "deals with motion and is not abstract," that is, its inquiry is centered on things that are in motion and are not abstracted from matter. He shows this by examples, as is clear in his treatise. His words "and the form that is joined with the matter takes on its movement" should be understood as follows: either the composite itself of matter and form, as such, has a movement appropriate to itself, or the form itself existing in matter is the principle of motion. So, one and the same inquiry concerns things insofar as they are material and insofar as they are in motion.

Next he explains the subject matter of mathematics, saying "Mathematics does not deal with motion," that is, unlike natural science it does not consider motion and mobile things, "and it is not abstract," that is, like natural science it considers forms which do

---

[7] See Aristotle, *Metaphysics* 6.1, 1026a18.

not exist separated from matter. He explains how this is possible. "For it," namely mathematics, "inquires into the forms of bodies apart from matter and therefore apart from motion," because wherever there is motion there is matter, as is proved in *Metaphysics* IX[8] (in the way in which there is motion there); and thus the inquiry of the mathematician is itself without matter and motion; "... which forms," namely those studied by the mathematician, "since they exist in matter, cannot be separated from bodies" in existence. So they are separable in thought but not in existence.

Then he shows what the object of the third science is, namely divine science. "Theology," that is, the third division of speculative science, which is called divine science or metaphysics or first philosophy, "does not deal with motion," being in this respect like mathematics and unlike natural science, "and it is abstract," namely from matter, "and inseparable,"[9] in both respect unlike mathematics. For divine things are abstract from matter and motion in their existence, but mathematicals are not abstract, though they are separable in thought. Divine things, however, are inseparable, for nothing is separable unless it is conjoined. Thus divine things are not separable from matter in thought, but they are abstract in existence, while the contrary is true of mathematicals. He proves this by the divine substance, which is the principal object of divine science, and therefore gives it its name.

Next, when he says "In the natural sciences, then," etc., he indicates the method appropriate to the divisions [of science] mentioned above. In this regard he makes two points. First, he states

---

[8] Ibid., 9.8, 1050b20-22. The reference is to the eternal local motion of the heavens.

[9] The text of Boethius reads *separabilis* (separable). See ed. Stewart-Rand-Tester, p. 8.15. St. Thomas' text read *inseparabilis*. See ed. Decker, p. 160.9; also p. 40, n. 1.

the methods suited to each of the above-mentioned divisions. We shall reserve the explanation of this to the disputation.[10] Second, he explains the last method, which is suited to the present investigation. He does this in two ways. First, he removes an impediment, saying "and in divine science we should not be turned aside to images," so that we follow the judgment of the imagination in forming our opinion about them. Second, he indicates what the appropriate [method] is when he says "but rather apprehend form itself" without motion and matter. The properties of this form he subsequently explains as he begins the proposed inquiry.[11]

---

[10] That is, the disputed questions that follow.

[11] Boethius describes the form apprehended in theology (i.e., God) as "pure form and no image, which is being itself (*esse ipsum*) and the source of being" (*De Trinitate*, c. 2; ed. Stewart-Rand-Tester, pp. 8.19-10.21).

Question Five

The Division of Speculative Science

There are two questions here.[1] The first concerns the division of speculative science which the text proposes,[2] the second concerns the methods it attributes to the parts of speculative science.

With regard to the first question there are four points of inquiry:

1. Is speculative science appropriately divided into these three parts: natural, mathematical, and divine?
2. Does natural philosophy treat of what exists in motion and matter?
3. Does mathematics treat, without motion and matter, of what exists in matter?
4. Does divine science treat of what exists without matter and motion?

ARTICLE ONE

Is Speculative Science Appropriately Divided into these Three Parts: Natural, Mathematical, and Divine?

We proceed as follows to the first article:

It seems that speculative science is not appropriately divided into these three parts, for

---

[1] The beginning of Chapter 2 of Boethius' *De Trinitate* (above, pp. 3-4), the point St. Thomas has reached in his Commentary.

[2] The text of Boethius, ibid.

1. The parts of speculative science are the habits that perfect the contemplative part of the soul. But the Philosopher says in the *Ethics*[3] that the scientific part of the soul, which is its contemplative part, is perfected by three habits, namely, wisdom, science, and understanding. Therefore these are the three divisions of speculative science, not those proposed in the text.[4]

2. Again, Augustine says[5] that rational philosophy, or logic, is included under contemplative or speculative philosophy. Consequently, since no mention is made of it, it seems the division is inadequate.

3. Again, philosophy is commonly divided into seven liberal arts, which include neither natural nor divine science, but only rational and mathematical science. Hence natural and divine should not be called parts of speculative science.

4. Again, medicine seems to be the most practical science, and yet it is said to contain a speculative part and a practical part. By the same token, therefore, all the other practical sciences have a speculative part. Consequently, even though it is a practical science, ethics or moral science should be mentioned in this division because of its speculative part.

5. Again, the science of medicine is a branch of physics, and similarly certain other arts called "mechanical," like the science of agriculture, alchemy, and others of the same sort. Therefore, since these sciences are practical, it seems that natural science should not be included without qualification under speculative science.

6. Again, a whole should not be contradistinguished from its part. But divine science seems to be a whole in relation to physics

---

[3] Aristotle, *Nicomachean Ethics* 6.3, 6 and 7, 1139b15-17, 1140b31-1141b8.
[4] The text of Boethius, ibid.
[5] St. Augustine, *De Civitate Dei* 8.4 (CSEL 40.1: 359).

and mathematics, since their subjects are parts of its subject. For the subject of divine science or first philosophy is being; and changeable substance, which the natural scientist considers, and also quantity, which the mathematician considers, are parts of being. This is clear in the *Metaphysics*.[6] Therefore, divine science should not be contradistinguished from natural science and mathematics.

7.   Again, as it is said in the *De Anima*,[7] sciences are divided in the same manner as things. But philosophy concerns being, for it is knowledge of being, as Dionysius says.[8] Now being is primarily divided into potency and act, one and many, substance and accident. So it seems that the parts of philosophy ought to be distinguished by such divisions of being.

8.   Again, there are many other divisions of beings studied by sciences more essential than the divisions into mobile and immobile and into abstract and non-abstract; for example, the divisions into corporeal and incorporeal and into living and non-living, and the like. Therefore differences of this sort should be the basis for the division of the parts of philosophy rather than those mentioned here.

9.   Again, that science on which others depend must be prior to them. Now all the other sciences depend on divine science because it is its business to prove their principles. Therefore Boethius should have placed divine science before the others.

10.   Again, mathematics should be studied before natural science, for the young can easily learn mathematics, but only the more advanced natural science, as is said in the *Ethics*.[9] This is why the ancients are said to have observed the following order in learning the sciences: first logic, then mathematics, then natural science, after

---

[6] Aristotle, *Metaphysics* 3.2, 997a26-30, b1-3.
[7] Aristotle, *De Anima* 3.8, 431b24.
[8] Pseudo-Dionysius, *Epistola* 7.2 (PG 3: 1080B).
[9] Aristotle, *Nicomachean Ethics* 6.8, 1142a11-20. See below, Appendix 3.2.

that moral science, and finally men studied divine science. Therefore, Boethius should have placed mathematics before natural science. And so it seems that this division is unsuitable.

On the contrary, the Philosopher proves the appropriateness of this division in the *Metaphysics*,[10] where he says, "There will be three philosophical and theoretical sciences: mathematics, physics, and theology."

Moreover, in the *Physics*[11] three methods of the sciences are proposed which indeed seem to belong to these three.

Moreover, Ptolemy also uses this division in the beginning of his *Almagest.*[12]

Reply: The theoretical or speculative intellect is properly distinguished from the operative or practical intellect by the fact that the speculative intellect has for its end the truth that it contemplates, while the practical intellect directs the truth under consideration to activity as to an end. So the Philosopher says in the *De Anima*[13] that they differ from each other by their ends; and in the *Metaphysics*[14] he states that "the end of speculative knowledge is truth, but the end of practical knowledge is action."

Now, since matter must be proportionate to the end, the subject-matter of the practical sciences must be things that can be made or done by us, so that we can direct the knowledge of them to activity as to an end.[15] On the other hand, the subject-matter of the

---

[10] Aristotle, *Metaphysics* 6.1, 1026a18.
[11] Aristotle, *Physics* 2.7, 198a29-31.
[12] Claudius Ptolemaeus, *Syntaxis Mathematica* 1.1 (*Opera Omnia* 1: 5, 7-10).
[13] Aristotle, *De Anima*, 3.10, 433a15.
[14] Aristotle, *Metaphysics* 2.1, 993b20.
[15] For the distinction between speculative and practical knowledge, see St. Thomas, *Summa Theol.* 1.1.4; 1.14.16; *De Veritate* 2, 8; 3, 3; *In I Eth.* lect. 1 and

speculative sciences must be things that cannot be made or done by us, so that our knowledge of them cannot be directed to activity as to an end. And the speculative sciences must differ according to the distinctions among these things.

Now we must realize that when habits or powers are differentiated by their objects they do not differ according to just any distinction among these objects, but according to the distinctions that are essential to the objects as objects.[16] For example, it is incidental to a sense object as such whether it be an animal or a plant. Accordingly, the distinction between the senses is not based upon this difference but rather upon the difference between color and sound. So the speculative sciences must be divided according to differences between objects of speculation, considered precisely as such. Now an object of this kind—namely, an object of a speculative power—derives one characteristic from the side of the power of intellect and another from the side of the habit of science that perfects the intellect. From the side of the intellect it has the fact that it is immaterial, because the intellect itself is immaterial. From the side of the habit of science it has the fact that it is necessary, for science treats of necessary matters, as is shown in the *Posterior Analytics*.[17] Now everything that is necessary is, as such, immobile, because everything changeable is, as such, able to be or not to be, either absolutely or in a certain respect, as is said in the *Metaphysics*.[18]

---

3. See also J. Maritain, *The Degrees of Knowledge*, pp. 311-315, Appendix VII, pp. 456-464; Yves Simon, *Critique de la connaissance morale*.

[16] For the distinction of powers and habits according to objects, see St. Thomas, *Summa Theol.* 1.77.3; 1-2.54.2; *In I Phys.* lect. 1, nn. 1-3, Eng. trans. p. 13.

[17] Aristotle, *Posterior Analytics*, 1.6, 74b5-75a37.

[18] Aristotle, *Metaphysics* 9.8, 1050b11-15. See St. Thomas, *In IX Meta.* lect. 9, n. 1869.

Consequently, separation from matter and motion, or connection[19] with them, essentially belongs to an object of speculation, which is the object of speculative science. As a result, the speculative sciences are differentiated according to their degree of separation from matter and motion.

Now there are some objects of speculation that depend on matter for their being, for they can exist only in matter. And these are subdivided. Some depend on matter both for their being and for their being understood, as do those things whose definition contains sensible matter and which, as a consequence, cannot be understood without sensible matter. For example, it is necessary to include flesh and bones in the definition of man. It is things of this sort that physics or natural science studies. On the other hand, there are some things that, although dependent upon matter for their being, do not depend upon it for their being understood, because sensible matter is not included in their definitions. This is the case with lines and numbers—the kind of objects with which mathematics deals. There are still other objects of speculative knowledge that do not depend upon matter for their being, because they can exist without matter; either they never exist in matter, as in the case of God and the angels, or they exist in matter in some instances and not in others, as in the case of substance, quality, being, potency, act, one and many, and the like. The science that treats of all these is theology or divine science, which is so called because its principal object is God. By another name it is called metaphysics; that is to say, *beyond physics*, because it ought to be learned by us after physics; for we

---

[19] *Applicatio.* St. Thomas here refers to the connection or relation between the universal natures considered by natural science and the individual things from which they are abstracted. This connection, known through an act of reflection, is necessary for natural science. See below, Q. 5, a. 2 and Reply to 4, pp. 30-31. See *In De Sensu et Sensato*, 1 (Paris, 1875), vol. 24, p. 198.

have to proceed from sensible things to those that are non-sensible. It is also called first philosophy,[20] inasmuch as all the other sciences, receiving their principles from it, come after it.[21] Now there can be nothing that depends upon matter for its being understood but not for its being, because by its very nature the intellect is immaterial. So there is no fourth kind of philosophy besides the ones mentioned.

Replies to the Opposing Arguments:

Reply to 1. In the *Ethics*,[22] the Philosopher considers the intellectual habits insofar as they are intellectual virtues. Now they are called virtues because they perfect the intellect in its operation; for

[20] See J. F. Wippel, *Metaphysical Themes in Thomas Aquinas*, ch. III: First Philosophy according to Thomas Aquinas, pp. 55-67. For a similar explanation of the three names of this science, see the *Prooemium* to St. Thomas' Commentary on the *Metaphysics*, trans. below, Appendix 2. Divine science and theology are here used as synonymous with metaphysics. They are not the theology of Sacred Scripture, as St. Thomas explains below in Q. 5, a. 4, pp. 52-53. Aristotle himself calls this science primary philosophy or theology. The name "metaphysics" does not come from him, but from either Andronicus of Rhodes or some earlier editor of Aristotle's works in the first century DC who placed the treatises on primary philosophy after the *Physics* and therefore called them the treatises after the *Physics*. It is also possible that the name was coined to signify that metaphysics goes beyond the order of physics. See W. Ross, *Aristotle's Metaphysics*, 1: xxxi-xxxii; W. Jaeger, *Aristotle*, pp. 378-379; J. Owens, *A History of Ancient Western Philosophy*, p. 290, n. 15.

[21] Of course the other sciences have their own proper principles, which can be known without an explicit knowledge of the principles of metaphysics. Hence these sciences do not directly depend on metaphysics; they are autonomous in their own spheres. Yet the principles of metaphysics are the absolutely universal and primary principles. All the others can be resolved into them. It is in this sense that all the other sciences are said to take their principles from metaphysics, and that this science is said to explain the principles of all the sciences. See below, Reply to 9, p. 23; Q. 6, a. 1, Reply to the Third Question, p. 73. See also *In I Post. Anal.* lect. 17, nn. 4-5; J. Maritain, *Introduction to Philosophy*, pp. 113-114.

[22] Aristotle, *Nicomachean Ethics* 6.3ff., 1139b14ff. For the quotation that follows, see ibid. 2.6, 1106a15-17.

"virtue makes its possessor good and renders his work good." So he distinguishes between virtues of this sort inasmuch as speculative habits perfect the intellect in different ways. In one way the speculative part of the soul is perfected by understanding, which is the habit of principles, through which some things become known of themselves. In another way it is perfected by a habit through which conclusions demonstrated from these principles are known, whether the demonstration proceeds from inferior causes, as in science, or from the highest causes, as in wisdom. But when sciences are differentiated insofar as they are habits, they must be distinguished according to their objects, that is, according to the things of which the sciences treat. And it is in this way that both here and in the *Metaphysics*[23] speculative philosophy is distinguished into three parts.

Reply to 2. As is evident in the beginning of the *Metaphysics*,[24] the speculative sciences concern things the knowledge of which is sought for their own sake. However, we do not seek to know the things studied by logic for themselves, but as a help to the other sciences. So logic is not included under speculative philosophy as a principal part but as something brought under speculative philosophy as furnishing speculative thought with its instruments, namely, syllogisms, definitions, and the like, which we need in the speculative sciences. Thus, according to Boethius,[25] logic is not so much a science as the instrument of science.

---

[23] Aristotle, *Metaphysics* 6.1, 1026a18.

[24] Ibid., 1.1, 981b13-21; 1.2, 982a14-17.

[25] Boethius, *In Isagogen Porphyrii Comm.*, ed. secunda, 1.3 (CSEL 48: 142); Eng. trans. p. 77.

Sometimes St. Thomas calls logic a science because it proceeds by demonstration. (See *In I Perih.* lect. 1, n. 2; *In I Post. Anal.* lect. 1, n. 2; *In IV Meta.* lect. 4, n. 576.) At other times he calls it an art, because it involves the construction of syllogisms and the like, and it has a practical purpose, namely the direction of the

Reply to 3. The seven liberal arts do not adequately divide theoretical philosophy; but, as Hugh of St. Victor says,[26] seven arts are grouped together (leaving out certain other ones), because those who wanted to learn philosophy were first instructed in them. And the reason why they are divided into the trivium and quadrivium[27] is that "they are as it were paths (*viae*) introducing the quick mind to the secrets of philosophy."[28] This is also in harmony with the Philosopher's statement in the *Metaphysics*,[29] that we must investigate the method of scientific thinking before the sciences themselves. And the Commentator says in the same place[30] that before all the other sciences a person should learn logic, which teaches the method of all the sciences; and the trivium concerns logic. The Philosopher also says in the *Ethics*[31] that the young can know

---

human reason in its movement toward truth. Art is defined as the determined ordination of reason by which human actions through determined means arrive at their due end. Logic is the art by which reason directs itself so that it will reach its due end, which is truth. Indeed, it is the "art of arts," because it directs reason itself, from which in turn all the arts proceed. See *In I Post. Anal.* lect. 1, nn. 1-3; John of St. Thomas, *Ars Logica* 2, Q. 1, a. 2, pp. 256ff.; J. Maritain, *Introduction to Philosophy,* pp. 142-148. See also below, note 41.

[26] Hugh of St. Victor, *Didascalion* 3.3, p. 52, l. 28 - p. 53, l. 8.

[27] The trivium contains grammar, rhetoric, and logic; the quadrivium arithmetic, geometry, astronomy, and music. Inherited from the classical culture of Rome through the writings of Cicero and Quintilian, they became the foundation of mediaeval education. See L. J. Paetow, *The Arts Course at Mediaeval Universities with Special Reference to Grammar and Rhetoric*; Hastings Rashdall, *The Universities of Europe in the Middle Ages,* ed. by F. M. Powicke and A. B. Emden, 1: 34-37; G. Paré, A. Brunet, P. Tremblay, *La Renaissance du XIIᵉ siècle,* pp. 98-108; R. McKeon, "Rhetoric in the Middle Ages," *Speculum* 17 (1942), 1-32.

[28] Hugh of St. Victor, ibid. Hugh of St. Victor is calling the reader's attention to the etymology of the words "tri*vium*" and "quadri*vium*."

[29] Aristotle, *Metaphysics* 2.3, 995a12-14.

[30] Averroes, *In II Meta.* 3, t. c. 15, fol. 35FG.

[31] Aristotle, *Nicomachean Ethics* 6.8, 1142a11-20.

mathematics but not physics, because it requires experience. So we are given to understand that after logic we should learn mathematics, which the quadrivium concerns. These, then, are like paths leading the mind to the other philosophical disciplines.

We may add that among the other sciences these are called arts because they involve not only knowledge but also a work that is directly a product of reason itself; for example, producing a composition,[32] syllogism or discourse, numbering, measuring, composing melodies, and reckoning the course of the stars. Other sciences (such as divine and natural science) either do not involve a work produced but only knowledge, and so we cannot call them arts, because, as the *Metaphysics* says,[33] art is "productive reason"; or they involve some bodily activity, as in the case of medicine, alchemy,[34] and other sciences of this kind. These latter, then, cannot be called liberal arts because such activity belongs to man on the side

---

[32] Translating *constructionem* in the grammatical sense of "composition." St. Thomas' examples are taken from the seven liberal arts: grammar, logic and rhetoric (the trivium), arithmetic, geometry, music and astronomy (the quadrivium). Another possible reading is *constructionem syllogismi* (the formation of a syllogism). This is parallel to *Summa Theol.* 1-2.57.3, ad 3.

[33] Aristotle, *Metaphysics* 6.1, 1025b22. Aristotle defines art as a habit that is directed to making and that involves a true course of reasoning. (See *Nicomachean Ethics* 6.4, 1140a10.) Following Aristotle, St. Thomas defines it as an operative habit accompanied by right reason. (See *In VI Ethic.* lect. 3, n. 1153.) Again, he says that art is nothing else than right reason about works to be made. (See *Summa Theol.* 1-2.57.3.) On this point, consult J. Maritain, *Art and Scholasticism*, p. 9.

[34] Alchemy is the art of transmuting base metals into pure ones, such as silver and gold. For the history of alchemy and its relation to chemistry, see F. Sherwood Taylor, *The Alchemists, Founders of Modern Chemistry.* St. Thomas' views on alchemy are treated on pp. 96-100, but they are drawn from the Commentary on Book 3 of the *Meteors*, which is not the work of St. Thomas but of his disciple, Peter of Auvergne. (See St. Thomas, *Opera Omnia*, ed. Leonine 3: xxxiii.) Lynn Thorndike draws from the same source in describing St. Thomas' views on alchemy. See his *A History of Magic and Experimental Science* 2: 607.

of his nature in which he is not free, namely, on the side of his body.[35] And although moral science is directed to action, still that action is not the act of the science but rather of virtue, as is clear in the *Ethics*.[36] So we cannot call moral science an art; but rather in these actions virtue takes the place of art. Thus, as Augustine says,[37] the ancients defined virtue as the art of noble and well-ordered living.

[35] For this reason they are called mechanical or servile arts, in distinction to the liberal arts, which, although they involve a work produced directly by reason itself, do not exist for the sake of that work, but rather are directed to knowledge. St. Thomas says, "Only those arts are called liberal which are directed to knowledge. Those directed to some utility to be achieved through action are called mechanical or servile." (*In 1 Meta.* lect. 3, n. 59.) "Even in speculative matters there is something by way of work: e.g., the making of a syllogism or of a fitting speech, or the work of counting or measuring. Hence whatever habits are directed to such works of the speculative reason are, by a kind of comparison, called arts indeed, but *liberal* arts, in order to distinguish them from those arts that are ordained to works done by the body; for these arts are, in a fashion, servile, inasmuch as the body is in servile subjection to the soul, and man, as regards his soul, is free [*liber*]." *Summa Theol.* 1-2.57.3, ad 3m. See M.-D. Chenu, "Arts 'mécaniques' et œuvres serviles," *Revue des sciences phil. et théol.* 29 (1940), 313-315.

[36] Aristotle, *Nicomachean Ethics* 6.13, 1144b17-30. There is a distinction between the moral science of right conduct and the moral virtues, which are the proximate principles of right conduct. Moral science or ethics is a practical science because its purpose is to direct human action; but it guides man only in a remote way, because as a science it deals with human actions in general and not directly with the particular action to be done here and now. The moral virtue of prudence is the immediate guide to action in the moral order. See J. Maritain, *The Degrees of Knowledge*, pp. 311-315, and Appendix VII, pp. 456-464; *Introduction to Philosophy*, pp. 264-267.

[37] St. Augustine, *De Civitate Dei* 4.21 (CSEL 40.1: 188); 19.1 (CSEL 40.2: 364). Referring to this statement of St. Augustine, J. Maritain says that the virtue of prudence, "which discerns and applies the means of attaining our moral ends," can be called an art only metaphorically. For art, in the proper sense of the word, is directed to the good work which the artist produces, whereas the virtue of prudence is directed to the good of the agent. See J. Maritain, *Art and Scholasticism*, p. 14.

Reply to 4. As Avicenna says,[38] the distinction between theoretical and practical is not the same when philosophy is divided into theoretical and practical, when the arts are divided into theoretical and practical, and when medicine is so divided. For when we distinguish philosophy or the arts into theoretical and practical we must do so on the basis of their end, calling that theoretical which is directed solely to knowledge of the truth, and that practical which is directed to operation. However, there is this difference when we distinguish the whole of philosophy and the arts on this basis: We divide philosophy with respect to the final end or happiness, to which the whole of human life is directed. For, as Augustine says,[39] following Varro, "There is no other reason for a man philosophizing except to be happy." And since the philosophers teach that there is a twofold happiness, one contemplative and the other active, as is clear in the *Ethics*,[40] they have accordingly also distinguished between two parts of philosophy, calling moral philosophy practical and natural and rational philosophy theoretical. But when they call some arts speculative and some practical, this is on the basis of some *special* ends of those arts; as when we say that agriculture is a practical art but dialectic is theoretical.[41]

However, when we divide medicine into theoretical and practical, the division is not on the basis of the end. For on that basis the

---

[38] Avicenna, *Canon Medicinae* 1, fen. 1, doctr. 1, prologus (Venice [1608], 1: 6, a 33-40).

[39] St. Augustine, *De Civitate Dei* 19.1 (CSEL 40.2: 366). St. Augustine refers to Varro's *Liber de Philosophia*, which is not extant.

[40] Aristotle, *Nicomachean Ethics* 10.7-8, 1177a12-1178b32.

[41] Logic or dialectic is not properly a speculative science, but rather a liberal art, since it is ordained to knowledge and it involves the construction of syllogisms, definitions, etc. (see above, note 35). But its special end is to serve the speculative sciences, of which it is the instrument. Hence it can be called speculative or theoretical by reduction (see above, note 25).

whole of medicine is practical, since it is directed to practice. But the above division is made on the basis of whether what is studied in medicine is proximate to, or remote from practice. Thus we call that part of medicine practical which teaches the method of healing; for instance, that these particular medicines should be given for these abscesses. On the other hand, we call that part theoretical which teaches the principles directing a man in his practice, although not immediately; for instance, that there are three virtues,[42] and that there are so many kinds of fever. Consequently, if we call some part of a practical science theoretical, we should not on that account place that part under speculative philosophy.

Reply to 5. One science is contained under another in two ways: in one way, as its part, because its subject is part of the subject of that other science, as plant is part of natural body. So the science of plants is also contained under natural science as one of its parts. In another way, one science is contained under another as subalternated to it. This occurs when in a higher science there is given the reason for what a lower science knows only as a fact.[43] This is how music is contained under arithmetic.

Medicine, therefore, is not contained under physics as a part, for the subject of medicine is not part of the subject of natural science

---

[42] St. Thomas refers to the classical division of virtues in medicine into vital, natural, and animal. See Avicenna, *Canon Medicinae* 1, fen. 1, doctr. 6 (Venice [1608], 1: 70, b 40-44).

[43] When one science is subalternated to another, it is inferior to it and borrows principles from it as from a superior science. It cannot explain those borrowed principles by itself. Only the higher science can do that. It assumes that they are true without knowing why they are true. For St. Thomas' doctrine of the subalternation of science, see *In Boetium de Trinitate* 2.2, Reply to 5; *In I Sent.* Prol. Q. 1, a. 3, quest. 3, sol. 2; *In I Post Anal.* lect. 25. See also John of St. Thomas, *Ars Logica* 2.26.2, pp. 795-802.

from the point of view from which it is the subject of medicine. For although the curable body is a natural body, it is not the subject of medicine insofar as it is curable by nature, but insofar as it is curable by art. But because art is nature's handmaid in healing (in which art too plays a part, for health is brought about through the power of nature with the assistance of art), it follows that the reason for the practices used in the art must be based on the properties of natural things. So medicine is subalternated to physics, and for the same reason so too are alchemy, the science of agriculture, and all sciences of this sort. We conclude, then, that physics in itself and in all its parts is speculative, although some practical sciences are subalternated to it.

Reply to 6.   Although the subjects[44] of the other sciences are parts of being, which is the subject of metaphysics, the other sciences are not necessarily parts of metaphysics. For each science treats of one part of being in a special way distinct from that in which metaphysics treats of being. So its subject is not properly speaking a part of the subject of metaphysics, for it is not a part of being from the point of view from which being is the subject of metaphysics; from this viewpoint it is a special science distinct from the others. However, the science treating of potency, or that treating of act or unity or anything of this sort, could be called a part of metaphysics, because these are considered in the same manner as being, which is the subject of metaphysics.

Reply to 7.   These parts of being require the same manner of consideration as being-in-general (*ens commune*) because they too are independent of matter. For this reason the science dealing with them is not distinct from the science of being-in-general.

---

[44] For the meaning of the subject of a science, see above, Introduction, p. xvii.

Reply to 8. The other diversities of things mentioned in the objection do not differentiate those things essentially as objects of knowledge. So the sciences are not distinguished according to them.

Reply to 9. Although divine science is by nature the first of all the sciences, with respect to us the other sciences come before it.[45] For, as Avicenna says,[46] the position of this science is that it be learned after the natural sciences, which explain many things used by metaphysics, such as generation, corruption, motion, and the like. It should also be learned after mathematics, because to know the separate substances metaphysics has to know the number and disposition of the heavenly spheres, and this is impossible without astronomy, which presupposes the whole of mathematics.[47] Other sciences, such as music, ethics, and the like, contribute to its fullness of perfection.

Nor is there necessarily a vicious circle because metaphysics presupposes conclusions proved in the other sciences while it itself proves their principles. For the principles that another science (such as natural philosophy) takes from first philosophy do not prove the

---

[45] See J. F. Wippel, "Aquinas and Avicenna on the Relationship between First Philosophy and the other Theoretical Sciences," in his *Metaphysical Themes in Thomas Aquinas,* pp. 35-53.

[46] Avicenna, *Metaphysics* 1.3; ed. Van Riet 1: 20.77-23.28.

[47] According to Aristotle, the separate substances or intelligences are the movers of the heavenly spheres and are equal in number to them. (See *Metaphysics* 12.8, 1073a32ff.) Although St. Thomas thought that the angels move the heavenly bodies, he does not restrict their number to the number of these bodies. See *Summa Theol.* 1.50.3; *De Substantiis Separatis* 2, ed. Leonine, p. D45.129-164; Eng. trans. pp. 47-50. See also below, Q. 5, a. 4, note 28.

In general, metaphysics uses the inferior sciences and in this sense depends on them. But this dependence is purely material. As the supreme science in the natural order, metaphysics is independent in its own sphere and does not exist for the sake of the other sciences. It is supremely free. See St. Thomas, *In I Meta.* lect. 3, n. 58; J. Maritain, *An Introduction to Philosophy,* p. 118.

points which the first philosopher takes from the natural philosopher, but they are proved through other self-evident principles. Similarly the first philosopher does not prove the principles he gives the natural philosopher by principles he receives from him, but by other self-evident principles. So there is no vicious circle in their definitions.

Moreover, the sensible effects on which the demonstrations of natural science are based are more evident to us in the beginning. But when we come to know the first causes through them, these causes will reveal to us the reason for the effects, from which they were proved by a demonstration *quia*.[48] In this way natural science also contributes something to divine science, and nevertheless it is divine science that explains its principles. That is why Boethius[49] places divine science last, because it is the last relative to us.

Reply to 10.   Although we should learn natural science after mathematics because the general proofs of natural science require experience and time, still, since natural things fall under the senses, they are by nature better known than the mathematical entities abstracted from sensible matter.

---

[48] A demonstration *quia* is one that proves the existence of something from its effect, without revealing the very nature of that thing or giving the reason why it is. Only a demonstration *propter quid* does that. Thus the demonstrations of the existence of God based on the sensible world are demonstrations *quia*, not *propter quid*. "Demonstrations can be made in two ways: one is through the cause, and is called *propter quid*, and this is to argue from what is prior absolutely. The other is through the effect, and this is called a demonstration *quia*; this is to argue from what is prior relatively only to us." *Summa Theol.* 1.2.2. See *Contra Gentiles* 1.12; *In I Post Anal.* lect. 23. See also G. Smith, *Natural Theology*, pp. 55-59.

[49] Boethius, *De Trinitate* 2, above, p. 3.

ARTICLE TWO

Does Natural Philosophy Treat of What Exists in Motion[1] and Matter?

We proceed as follows to the second article:

It seems that natural science does not treat of things that exist in motion and matter, for

1. Matter is the principle of individuation. Now, according to Plato's doctrine, which is followed by Porphyry,[2] no science treats of individual things but only of universals. Therefore, natural science does not treat of what is in matter.

2. Again, science pertains to the intellect. But the intellect knows by abstracting from matter and from the conditions of matter. Therefore, no science can treat of what is not abstracted from matter.

3. Again, as is clear in the *Physics*,[3] the First Mover is considered in natural science. But the First Mover is free from all matter. Therefore, natural science does not treat only of what is in matter.

4. Again, every science has to do with what is necessary. But whatever is moved, as such is contingent, as is proved in the *Metaphysics*.[4] Therefore, no science can treat of what is subject to motion; and so neither can natural science.

5. Again, no universal is subject to motion; for as is said in the beginning of the *Metaphysics*,[5] it is not man in general who is healed,

---

[1] Motion (*motus*), as used throughout the article, means not only change of place, but change in general, including qualitative, quantitative, and substantial change. For St. Thomas' doctrine of change, see *In III Phys.* lect. 1-5; Eng. trans. pp. 7, 28-49.

[2] Porphyry, *Isagoge* (*Commentaria in Aristotl. Graeca* 4/1, p. 6, 12-16); Eng. trans. p. 40.17-18. See Plato, *Philebus* 16C-D, 17D; *Laches* 198D.

[3] Aristotle, *Physics* 8.5, 256a4-260a19, 266a10-267b26.

[4] Aristotle, *Metaphysics* 9.8, 1050b11-15.

[5] Aristotle, *Metaphysics* 1.1, 981a18-20.

but *this* man. But every science concerns that which is universal. Therefore natural science does not treat of what is in motion.

6.   Again, some of the things with which natural science deals are not subject to motion; for instance, the soul, as is shown in the *De Anima*,[6] and the earth, as is proved in the *De Caelo et Mundo*.[7] What is more, all natural forms neither come into being nor perish, and for the same reason they are not subject to motion, except accidentally. This is shown in the *Metaphysics*.[8] Therefore not everything that physics considers is in motion.

7.   Again, every creature is mutable for, as Augustine says,[9] true immutability belongs to God alone. So if it is the task of natural science to consider what is in motion, it will be its business to consider all creatures, which clearly appears to be false.

On the contrary, it is the work of natural science to reach conclusions about natural things. Now, natural things are those in which there is a principle of motion; and, as the *Metaphysics* says,[10] wherever there is motion there must be matter. So natural science treats of what is in motion and matter.

Moreover, there must be some speculative science dealing with what is in matter and motion, for otherwise the teaching of philosophy, which is knowledge of being, would be incomplete. Now no other speculative science treats of these things, for neither mathematics nor metaphysics does so. Therefore, natural science treats of them.

---

[6] Aristotle, *De Anima* 1.3, 405b31-407b26.

[7] Aristotle, *De Caelo et Mundo* 2.14, 296a24-297a6. For the immobility of the earth, see below, note 25.

[8] Aristotle, *Metaphysics* 7.8, 1033b5-7.

[9] St. Augustine, *De Civitate Dei* 11.10 (CSEL 40.1: 525); *De Trinitate* 5.2, n. 3 (PL 42: 912).

[10] Aristotle, *Metaphysics* 9.8, 1050b22; see 7.8, 1033b18.

Moreover, the fact is clear from the statements of the Philosopher in the *Metaphysics*[11] and the *Physics*.[12]

Reply: It was the difficulty of this problem that drove Plato to posit Ideas. Believing that all sensible things were always in flux, as Cratylus and Heraclitus taught, he thought there can be no science concerning them, as the Philosopher says in the *Metaphysics*.[13] So he claimed that there were substances separated from the sense world, which might serve as the objects of science and of definitions. He made this mistake because he failed to distinguish what is essential from what is accidental. For it happens that by accident even the wise often fall into error, as is said in the *Sophistic Refutations*.[14]

Now, as is shown in the *Metaphysics*,[15] we find in a sensible substance both the whole or the composite itself, and also its nature (*ratio*) or form;[16] and it is the composite that is essentially generated and corrupted and not the nature or form, except accidentally. As

---

[11] Aristotle, *Metaphysics* 6.1, 1025b26-28; 1026a13.

[12] Aristotle, *Physics* 2.2, 193b22-194a12.

[13] Aristotle, *Metaphysics* 1.6, 987a32-34.

[14] Aristotle, *Sophistic Refutations* 1.6, 168b6-8.

[15] Aristotle, *Metaphysics* 7.15, 1039b20 24.

[16] Form, as used here by St. Thomas, means the whole nature or essence of a thing. It is the *ratio* of a thing, or that which its definition signifies. For example, humanity is the essence of Peter; consequently it is his form or *ratio*. Notice that form in this context does not mean substantial form, for instance, the soul of man. The difference between these two meanings of the word "form" is expressed by the terms *forma totius* (form of the whole) and *forma partis* (form of the part). The former is the whole essence, including both form and matter in a material substance. The latter is a part of the essence and excludes matter. See St. Thomas, *De Ente et Essentia* 2, ed. Leonine pp. 370.1-371.66, 373.274-291, Eng. trans. pp. 31, 43-44; *In VII Meta.* lect. 9, nn. 1467-1469. See also A. Maurer, "Form and Essence in the Philosophy of St. Thomas," in *Mediaeval Studies* 13 (1951), 165-176.

the *Metaphysics* says,[17] "It is not *house* that is made, but *this house*."
Now anything can be thought of without all the items that are not
essentially related to it. Consequently, forms and natures, though
belonging to things existing in motion, are without motion when
they are considered in themselves; and so they can be the objects of
sciences and of definitions, as the Philosopher says.[18] As he proves,[19]
the sciences of sensible reality are not based upon the knowledge of
certain substances separated from the sense world.

Natures of this kind, which are the objects of the sciences of real
beings, are thought of without motion; and so they must be thought
of without those conditions by reason of which motion belongs to
mobile things. Now, because every motion is measured by time, and
the primary motion is local motion (for without it there is no other
motion), a thing must be subject to motion inasmuch as it exists here
and now; and it exists under these conditions insofar as it is
individuated by matter having determinate dimensions.[20] Consequently, natures of this kind, which make possible sciences of things
subject to motion, must be thought of without determinate matter
and everything following upon such matter; but not without inde-

[17]   Aristotle, *Metaphysics* 7.15, 1039b25.
[18]   Aristotle, *Metaphysics* 7.15, 1039b27-1040a2. Aristotle shows here that there
is neither scientific definition nor demonstration about sensible individual substances because they are contingent. Science deals primarily with the necessary, for
example, with the natures of things as defined in universal concepts. See St.
Thomas, *In VII Meta.* lect. 15. For the way in which the individual is known in
natural science, see below, Q. 5, a. 2, Reply to 4, pp. 30-31.
[19]   Aristotle, *Metaphysics* 7.14, 1039a24ff.
[20]   For St. Thomas' doctrine of individuation of form by matter, see Roland-
Gosselin, *Le "De Ente et Essentia,"* pp. 104-126. By determinate matter (*materia
signata*) is meant particular matter, for instance, *this* flesh or *these* bones. By
indeterminate matter is meant common matter, for instance, flesh and bones. The
natures studied by natural sciences abstract from the former, but not from the latter
kind of matter. See *Summa Theol.* 1.85.1, ad 2[m].

terminate matter, because on its notion depends the notion of form that determines matter to itself. Thus the nature of man, which his definition signifies and which is the object of science, is considered without *this* flesh and *these* bones, but not absolutely without flesh and bones. And because individuals include determinate matter in their nature, whereas universals include common matter, as is said in the *Metaphysics*,[21] the above-mentioned abstraction is not said to be the abstraction of form from matter absolutely, but the abstraction of the universal from the particular.

Natures of this sort, thus abstracted, can be considered in two ways. First, in themselves; and then they are thought of without motion and determinate matter. This happens to them only by reason of the being they have in the intellect. Second, they can be viewed in relation to the things of which they are the natures; and these things exist with matter and motion. Thus they are principles by which we know these things, for everything is known through its form. Consequently, in natural science we know mutable and material things existing outside the soul through natures of this kind; that is to say, natures that are immobile and considered without particular matter.

Replies to Opposing Arguments:

Reply to 1. Matter is the principle of individuation only insofar as it exists with determinate dimensions; and in this sense natural science indeed abstracts from matter.

Reply to 2. The intelligible form is a thing's quiddity, for, as the *De Anima* says,[22] the object of the intellect is the quiddity of a thing.

---

[21] Aristotle, *Metaphysics* 7.10, 1035b27-31.
[22] Aristotle, *De Anima* 3.6, 430b28. See St. Thomas, *In III De Anima*, lect. 8, nn. 705-717; Eng. trans. pp. 414-419.

Now, as is said in the *Metaphysics*,[23] the quiddity of a universal composite, like *man* or *animal*, includes within itself common but not particular matter. So the intellect regularly abstracts from determinate matter and its conditions; but in natural science it does not abstract from common matter, although matter itself is considered in natural science only in relation to form. For this reason the natural scientist is more concerned with form than with matter.

Reply to 3. Natural science does not treat of the First Mover as its subject or as part of its subject, but as the end to which natural science leads. Now the end does not belong to the nature of the thing of which it is the end, but it has a relation to it; as the end of a line is not the line but is related to it. So also the First Mover is of a different nature from natural things, but it is related to them because it moves them. So it falls under the consideration of natural science, not in itself, but insofar as it is a mover.

Reply to 4. Science treats of something in two ways: in one way, primarily and principally; and in this sense science is concerned with universal natures, which are its very foundation. In another way it treats of something secondarily, as by a sort of reflection; and in this sense it is concerned with the things whose natures they are, inasmuch as, using the lower powers, it relates those natures to the particular things possessing them. For a knower uses a universal nature both as a thing known and as a means of knowing. Thus, through the universal nature of man we can judge of this or that particular man. Now, all universal natures of things are immutable; and so, in this respect, all science is concerned with what is necessary. But some of the things possessing these natures are necessary and immutable, whereas others are contingent and subject

[23] Aristotle, *Metaphysics* 7.10, 1035b27-31.

to movement; and in this respect sciences are said to be concerned with the contingent and mutable.[24]

Reply to 5.   Although a universal is not mutable, it is nevertheless the nature of a mutable thing.

Reply to 6.   Although the soul and other natural forms are not themselves subject to motion, they are moved accidentally, and they are, moreover, the perfections of mutable things; and for this reason they come within the domain of natural science. But even though the earth as a whole is not moved (for it happens to be in its natural place, where a thing is at rest in virtue of the same nature through which it is moved to a place), nevertheless, when its parts are outside their proper place, they are moved to a place.[25] Thus the earth falls within the domain of natural science both by reason of the immobility of the whole earth and by reason of the movement of its parts.

Reply to 7.   The mutability characteristic of all creatures is not with respect to any natural motion, but with respect to their dependence on God, separation from whom entails destruction of their very being. And that dependence falls under the consideration of metaphysics rather than under that of natural philosophy. Spiritual creatures, moreover, are mutable only with regard to choice; and this sort of motion is not the concern of the natural philosopher but rather of the metaphysician.

[24] Individual things are thus indirectly and secondarily the object of science. See above Reply, p. 28; also *Summa Theol.* 1.86.1; 1.86.3.

[25] According to mediaeval physics, each of the four elements, earth, water, air, and fire, has its natural place in the universe, with earth at the center. By virtue of its nature, each of the elements rests in its proper place in the order in which they are listed above, or if removed from that place tends to move back to it. That is why a stone, in which the element of earth predominates, tends to fall, and fire tends to rise. See St. Thomas, *In I De Caelo et Mundo,* lect. 17-18. See also J. de Tonquédec, *Questions de cosmologie et de physique chez Aristote et saint Thomas,* pp. 8-16.

For the immobility of the earth in the center of the universe, see St. Thomas, *In II De Caelo et Mundo,* lect. 21.

ARTICLE THREE

Does Mathematics Treat, Without Motion and Matter,
of What Exists in Matter?

We proceed as follows to the third article:

It seems that mathematical thinking does not treat, without motion and matter, of what exists in matter, for

1. Since truth consists in the conformity of thing to intellect, there must be falsehood whenever we think of something otherwise than it is. If then in mathematics we consider what is in matter in abstraction from matter, we will consider it falsely; and so mathematics will not be a science, for every science is concerned with what is true.

2. Again, as the Philosopher states,[1] every science has the task of considering a subject and the parts of the subject. Now in actual existence matter is a part of all material things. So it is impossible for a science to treat of what is in matter without treating of matter.

3. Again, all straight lines are specifically the same. But the mathematician treats of straight lines by numbering them; otherwise he would not treat of the triangle and the square. It follows that he considers lines as specifically the same and numerically different. But it is clear from the above that matter is the principle differentiating things specifically the same. So the mathematician treats of matter.

4. Again, no science completely abstracting from matter demonstrates through a material cause. But in mathematics some demonstrations are made which can only be reduced to a material cause, as when we demonstrate something about a whole by its parts. For, as the *Physics* says,[2] parts are the matter of the whole. Thus in

---

[1] Aristotle, *Posterior Analytics* 1.10, 76b11-16; 1.28, 87a38-39.
[2] Aristotle, *Physics* 2.3, 195a20.

the *Posterior Analytics*³ the demonstration that the angle in a semi-circle is a right angle from the fact that each of its two parts is half of a right angle, is reduced to a material cause. Therefore, mathematics does not entirely abstract from matter.

5.   Again, motion cannot exist without matter. But the mathematician ought to consider motion, because, since motion is measured relative to space, to consider the quantity of space, which pertains to the mathematician, and the quantity of motion, has the same nature and belongs to the same science. Therefore, the mathematician does not entirely leave matter out of consideration.

6.   Again, astronomy is a part of mathematics, and so too is the science of the moved sphere, the science of weights, and music,⁴ all of which treat of motion and mobile things. So mathematics does not entirely abstract from matter and motion.

7.   Again, natural science is entirely concerned with matter and motion. But some conclusions are demonstrated alike by the mathematician and the natural scientist; for instance, whether the earth is round and whether it is in the middle of the universe. Therefore, mathematics cannot entirely abstract from matter.

If it be said that mathematics abstracts only from sensible matter, the contrary seems true. Sensible matter seems to be particular matter, because what the senses perceive are particular things, and all the sciences abstract from this kind of matter. So mathematical thinking should not be called more abstract than that of the other sciences.

---

³ Aristotle, *Posterior Analytics* 2.11, 94a28-34.

⁴ See St. Thomas' reply to the argument for the sense in which these sciences are said to be parts of mathematics. By the science of the moved sphere (*sphaera mota*) is meant the general study of the movement of spherical bodies. See St. Thomas, *In VI Phys.* lect. 12, n. 3; see also the references to "moved sphere" in the Index to St. Thomas' Commentary on the *De Caelo et Mundo* in the Leonine edition, p. 443.

8.   Again, the Philosopher says[5] that there are three branches of study: the first concerns what is mutable and corruptible, the second what is mutable and incorruptible, and the third what is immutable and incorruptible. As Ptolemy explains,[6] the first is natural science, the third divine science, and the second mathematics. Therefore, mathematics concerns what is mutable.

To the contrary is the Philosopher's statement in the *Metaphysics.*[7]

Moreover, some things, although existing in matter, do not contain matter in their definition; for instance, *curve,* which differs in this respect from *snub.* Now philosophy should treat of all beings. Hence some part of philosophy must consider beings of this sort; and this is mathematics, for this does not belong to any other part.

Moreover, what is prior from the point of view of the intellect can be considered without what is posterior. Now mathematicals are prior to natural things existing in matter and motion, for the latter are so related to mathematicals that they add something to them, as is said in the *De Caelo et Mundo.*[8] Therefore, mathematical investigation can be without matter and motion.

Reply: In order to throw light on this question we must understand how the intellect in its operation is able to abstract.[9]

We must realize that, as the Philosopher says,[10] the intellect has two operations: one called the "understanding of indivisibles," by which it knows *what* a thing is, and another by which it joins and

---

[5] Aristotle, *Physics* 2.7, 198a28-31.
[6] Claudius Ptolemaeus, *Syntaxis Mathematica* 1.1 (*Opera Omnia* 1: 5.13-6.5).
[7] Aristotle, *Metaphysics* 6.1, 1026a7-10, 14.
[8] Aristotle, *De Caelo et Mundo* 3.1, 299a16.
[9] For the meaning of abstraction and the modes of abstraction, see above, Introduction, pp. xviii-xxxi.
[10] Aristotle, *De Anima* 3.6, 430a26-28.

divides, that is to say, by forming affirmative and negative statements. Now these two operations correspond to two principles in things.[11] The first operation concerns the nature itself of a thing, in virtue of which the object known holds a certain rank among beings, whether it be a complete thing, like some whole, or an incomplete thing, like a part or an accident. The second operation has to do with a thing's being (*esse*), which results from the union of the principles of a thing in composite substances, or, as in the case of simple substances, accompanies the thing's simple nature.

Now, since the truth of the intellect results from its conformity with reality, it is clear that in this second operation the intellect cannot truthfully abstract what is united in reality, because the abstraction would signify a separation with regard to the very being of the thing. For example, if I abstract man from whiteness by saying, "Man is not white," I signify that there is a separation in reality. So if in reality man and whiteness are not separate, the intellect will be false. Through this operation, then, the intellect can truthfully abstract only those things that are separate in reality, as when we say, "Man is not an ass."

Through the first operation, however, we can abstract things that are not separate in reality; not all, it is true, but some. For, since everything is intelligible insofar as it is in act, as the *Metaphysics* says,[12] we must understand the nature itself or the quiddity of a thing

---

[11] For parallel statements by St. Thomas, see *In I Sent.*, d. 19, q. 5, a. 1, ad 7, ed. Mandonnet, 1: 489; d. 38, q. 1, a. 3, sol., p. 903. See E. Gilson, *Being and Some Philosophers*, pp. 190-215; J. Owens, *An Elementary Christian Metaphysics*, pp. 45-56, 248-258; idem, *An Interpretation of Existence*, pp. 14-43; idem, "Aquinas on Knowing Existence," *The Review of Metaphysics* 29 (1976), 670-690. On the experience of being, see E. Gilson, *Constantes philosophiques de l'être*, c. VI: Rencontre de l'être, pp. 143-168.

[12] Aristotle, *Metaphysics* 9.9, 1051a30-32.

either inasmuch as it is a certain act (as happens in the case of forms themselves and simple substances); or through that which is its act (as we know composite substances through their forms); or through that which takes the place of act in it (as we know prime matter through its relation to form, and a vacuum through the absence of a body in place). And it is from this that each nature is given its definition.

Therefore, when the nature itself is related to, and depends on something else, with regard to that which forms the definition (*ratio*)[13] of the nature, and through which the nature itself is understood, clearly we cannot know the nature without that other thing. This is true whether they are connected as a part is united to a whole (as we cannot know *foot* without knowing *animal*, because that whereby *foot* has the nature of *foot* depends on that whereby *animal* is *animal*); or whether they are connected as form is united to matter, or as one part to another part, or as accident to subject (as we cannot know *snub* without *nose*); or even whether they are separated in reality (as we cannot know *father* without knowing *son*, although these relationships are found in different things). But if one thing does not depend on another with regard to that which forms the definition of the nature, then the intellect can abstract the one from the other so as to know it without the other. This is true not only if they are separated in reality, like *man* and *stone*, but also if they are united in reality, whether they are joined as part and whole (as *letter* can be understood without *syllable*, but not vice versa, and *animal* without *foot*, but not conversely); or even if they are joined

---

[13] The *ratio* of a thing is its definition, or, in other words, the concept that expresses what a thing is. By extension, the term also signifies the intelligible nature of a thing corresponding to its definition. More generally, *ratio* is simply what the intellect grasps of the meaning of any name. See St. Thomas, *In I Sent* 2.1.3; 33.1.1, ad 3ᵐ.

as form is united to matter and accident to subject (as *whiteness* can be understood without *man* and vice versa).

Accordingly, through its various operations the intellect distinguishes one thing from another in different ways. Through the operation by which it composes and divides, it distinguishes one thing from another by understanding that the one does not exist in the other. Through the operation, however, by which it understands what a thing is, it distinguishes one thing from another by knowing what one is without knowing anything of the other, either that it is united to it or separated from it. So this distinction is not properly called separation, but only the first. It is correctly called abstraction, but only when the objects, one of which is known without the other, are one in reality. For if we consider animal without considering stone, we do not say that we abstract animal from stone.

It follows that since, properly speaking, we can only abstract objects united in existence, there are two sorts of abstraction[14] corresponding to the two modes of union mentioned above, namely, the union of part and whole, and the union of form and matter. The first is that in which we abstract form from matter, and the second is that in which we abstract a whole from its parts.

Now a form can be abstracted from matter if the essential nature of the form does not depend on that particular kind of matter; but the intellect cannot abstract form from the kind of matter upon which the form depends according to its essential nature. Consequently, because all accidents are related to the underlying substance as form to matter, and because it is the nature of every accident to depend upon substance, no form of this kind can be separated from substance. But accidents befall substance in a definite order. Quantity

---

[14] See *De Substantiis Separatis* 1, ed. Leonine, p. D42.80-94; Eng. trans. pp. 38-39.

comes to it first, then quality, after that passivities (*passiones*) and actions. So quantity can be thought of in substance before the sensible qualities (because of which matter is called sensible) are considered in it. Quantity, then, according to its essential nature does not depend upon sensible matter but only upon intelligible matter.[15] For, after accidents have been abstracted, substance is intelligible only to the intellect, because it is beyond the sense powers to comprehend substance.[16] And abstract objects of this kind

[15] The matter that is the subject of mathematics is called "intelligible" because it is not perceived by the external senses, like "sensible matter," but by the imagination, which was sometimes called "intellect" by the mediaevals. See St. Thomas, *In VII Meta.* lect. 10, nn. 1494-1496; *In III De Anima*, lect. 10, n. 745; Eng. trans. p. 432.

Intelligible matter is defined as "substance as subject to quantity." See *Summa Theol.* 1.85.1, ad 2^m; *In II Phys.* lect. 3, n. 5. However, St. Thomas sometimes speaks of the subject of mathematics as simply quantities and their properties, such as figures, surface, and the like. (See *In VII Meta.* lect. 11, n. 1508.) It should be noticed that according to St. Thomas mathematics in a sense considers *qualities*, understood as formal determinations and relations of quantity. See *In V Meta.* lect. 16, nn. 989-992; *In VIII Meta.* lect. 5, n. 1761; J. Maritain, *The Degrees of Knowledge*, p. 35, n. 3.

[16] Throughout this question and Q. VI, a. 1, St. Thomas gives the impression that the object of mathematics is real quantity, known in abstraction from the sensible qualities of bodies. This has led some to the opinion that for St. Thomas mathematics is "not a study of an ideal order but a science of the real world" (V. Smith, *St. Thomas on the Object of Geometry*, p. 65). But as J. Maritain points out, mathematical entities acquire an ideal purity in the world of the mathematician that they do not have in real existence; see J. Maritain, *The Degrees of Knowledge*, pp. 166-167. Mathematical objects have properties that are not those of natural things; e.g., "that a straight line touches a sphere at only one point is true of an abstract straight line but not of a straight line in matter" (Q. VI, a. 2, p. 78). In his commentary on the *Sentences*, 1, d. 2, q. 1, a. 3, ed. Mandonnet 1: 67, St. Thomas places mathematical abstractions with logic as having only a remote foundation in reality. Their proximate foundation is the activity of the mind itself. See A. Maurer, "A Neglected Thomistic Text on the Foundation of Mathematics," *Mediaeval Studies* 21 (1959), 185-192.

According to the recent Leonine edition of St. Thomas' Commentary on the

are the concern of mathematics; it treats of quantities and the properties of quantity, such as figures and the like.

Moreover, we cannot abstract a whole from just any parts. For there are some parts upon which the nature of the whole depends, namely, when the being of a particular whole consists in the composition of particular parts. It is in this way that a syllable is related to letters and a mixed body to the elements. Parts of this sort, which are necessary for understanding the whole because they enter into its definition, are called parts of the species and of the form. There are some parts, however, that are accidental to the whole as such. The semicircle, for instance, is related to the circle in this way, for it is accidental to a circle that it be divided into two or more equal or unequal parts. But it is not accidental to a triangle that three lines are designated in it, for because of this a triangle is a triangle. Similarly, it is an essential characteristic of man that there be found in him a rational soul and a body composed of the four elements. So man cannot be understood without these parts and they must be included in his definition; so they are parts of his species and form. But finger, foot, and hand, and other parts of this kind are outside the definition of man; and thus the essential nature of man does not depend on them and he can be understood without them. For whether or not he has feet, as long as he is constituted of a rational soul and a body composed of the elements in the proper mixture required by this sort of form, he will be a man. These parts are called parts of matter: they are not included in the definition of the whole, but rather the converse is true. This is how all determinate (*signatae*) parts are related to man; for instance, *this* soul, *this* body, *this* nail,

---

Ethics, both mathematics and metaphysics are included under natural philosophy. See below, Appendix 1. But this is in the context of a current division of the sciences of Stoic origin that he does not adopt elsewhere.

this bone, etc. These indeed are parts of the essence of Socrates and
Plato, but not of man precisely as man; and therefore the intellect
can abstract man from these parts. And this is the abstraction of the
universal from the particular.

So there are two abstractions of the intellect. One corresponds to
the union of form and matter or accident and subject. This is the
abstraction of form from sensible matter. The other corresponds to
the union of whole and part; and to this corresponds the abstraction
of the universal from the particular. This is the abstraction of a
whole, in which we consider a nature absolutely, according to its
essential character, in independence of all parts that do not belong
to the species but are accidental parts. But we do not find abstractions opposed to these, by which a part is abstracted from a whole
or matter from form, because a part either cannot be abstracted from
a whole by the intellect if it is one of the parts of matter in whose
definition the whole is included; or it can even exist without the
whole if it is one of the parts of the species; for instance, a line
without a triangle, a letter without a syllable, or an element without
a mixed body. But in the case of things that can exist separately,
separation rather than abstraction obtains. Similarly, when we say
form is abstracted from matter, we do not mean substantial form,
because substantial form and the matter correlative to it are interde-
pendent, so that one is not intelligible without the other, because the
appropriate act is in its appropriate matter. Rather, we mean the
accidental forms of quantity and figure, from which indeed sensible
matter cannot be abstracted by the intellect, because sensible qualities cannot be understood unless quantity is presupposed, as is clear
in the case of surface and color. And neither can we understand
something to be the subject of motion unless we understand it to
possess quantity. Substance, however, which is the intelligible matter
of quantity, can exist without quantity. Consequently, the conside-

ration of substance without quantity belongs to the order of separation rather than to that of abstraction.

We conclude that there are three kinds of distinction in the operation of the intellect. There is one through the operation of the intellect joining and dividing which is properly called separation; and this belongs to divine science or metaphysics. There is another through the operation by which the quiddities of things are conceived which is the abstraction of form from sensible matter; and this belongs to mathematics. And there is a third through the same operation which is the abstraction of a universal from a particular; and this belongs to physics and to all the sciences in general, because science disregards accidental features and treats of necessary matters. And because certain men (for example, the Pythagoreans and the Platonists) did not understand the difference between the last two kinds of distinction and the first, they fell into error, asserting that the objects of mathematics and universals exist separate from sensible things.[17]

Replies to Opposing Arguments:

Reply to 1. When the mathematician abstracts he does not consider something otherwise than it is. Thus, he does not think that a line exists without sensible matter, but he treats of a line and its properties without considering sensible matter. So there is no disagreement between his intellect and reality, because even in reality what belongs to the nature of a line does not depend upon that which makes matter sensible, but vice versa. Consequently, it is evident that "there is no error in the one who abstracts," as is said in the *Physics.*[18]

---

[17] See St. Thomas, *Summa Theol.* 1.85.1, ad 1[m], 2[m].

[18] Aristotle, *Physics* 2.2, 193b35.

Reply to 2. By "material" is meant not only that which has matter as a part, but also that which exists in matter; and in this way a sensible line can be called something material. So this does not prevent a line from being understood without matter. For sensible matter is not related to a line as a part, but rather as the subject in which it exists, and this is also the case with a surface or body. Obviously, the mathematician does not treat of the kind of body that is in the category of substance, whose parts are matter and form, but rather the body in the category of quantity, constituted by three dimensions.[19] Body, in this sense of the term, is related to body in the category of substance (of which physical matter is a part) as an accident to its subject.

Reply to 3. Matter is the principle of numerical diversity only inasmuch as, being divided into many parts, and receiving in each part a form of the same nature, it constitutes many individuals of the same species. Now matter can be divided only if we presuppose quantity in it; if that is taken away, every substance remains indivisible. So the primary reason for the diversification of things of one species lies in quantity. And this is due to quantity because position, which is the arrangement of parts in place, is contained in its notion as a kind of formal difference. So even when the intellect has abstracted quantity from sensible matter, it is still possible to imagine numerically different things in the same species, for example, several equilateral triangles and several equal straight lines.

Reply to 4. Mathematics does not abstract from every kind of matter but only from sensible matter. Now the parts of quantity that seem to be in a way the basis for a demonstration by means of a material cause are not sensible matter; rather, they pertain to intel-

[19] For the meaning of the two senses of the term "body," see St. Thomas, *De Ente et Essentia,* 2, ed. Leonine, pp. 371.105-372.150; Eng. trans. pp. 38-40.

ligible matter, which indeed is found in mathematics, as is clear in the *Metaphysics.*[20]

Reply to 5. By its very nature motion is not in the category of quantity, but it partakes somewhat of the nature of quantity from another source, namely, according as the division of motion derives from either the division of space or the division of the thing subject to motion. So it does not belong to the mathematician to treat of motion, although mathematical principles can be applied to motion. Therefore, inasmuch as the principles of quantity are applied to motion, the natural scientist treats of the division and continuity of motion, as is clear in the *Physics.*[21] And the measurements of motions are studied in the intermediate sciences between mathematics and natural science;[22] for instance, in the science of the moved sphere[23] and in astronomy.[24]

[20] Aristotle, *Metaphysics* 7.10, 1036a11.

[21] Aristotle, *Physics* 6.4, 234b21-235b5.

[22] For the meaning of intermediate science (*scientia media*), see below, Replies to 6 and 7; also *In II Phys.* lect. 3, n. 8; *Summa Theol.* 2-2.9.2, ad 3ᵐ; *In I Post Anal.* lect. 25, n. 2. See also J. Maritain, *The Degrees of Knowledge,* pp. 41-42, 60-63, 138; *Réflexions sur l'intelligence,* pp. 186-187; *Philosophy of Nature,* pp. 36-44; *Science and Wisdom,* pp. 40-46.

Both in the present work and in the *Summa Theologiae* the intermediate sciences are said to have a greater affinity to mathematics than to physical science, since they are *formally* mathematical (that is, their method of demonstration is mathematical) and only *materially* physical (that is, the subject matter considered is sensible nature). In his Commentary on the *Physics,* however, he says that these sciences are more physical than mathematical because their *end* is sensible nature (that is, they purpose to study the physical universe, although by means of mathematics). Aristotle himself considered them parts of mathematics, although *the more physical parts.* (See Aristotle, *Physics* 2.2, 194a7-8.) The mediaeval Latin version of the *Physics* mistranslates the text of Aristotle to read that these sciences are *more physical than mathematical.* This, however, is not Aristotle's view. (See the Latin version of Aristotle's *Physics* in St. Thomas, *Opera Omnia,* ed. Leonine 2: 61.) For Aristotle's doctrine of these sciences, see Sir Thomas Heath, *Mathematics in Aristotle,* pp. 11-16.

Reply to 6.   Simple bodies and their properties remain in composite bodies although in a different way, as the proper qualities of the elements and their proper movements are found in a mixed body. What is proper to composite bodies, however, is not found in simple bodies. And so it is that the more abstract and simple the objects of a science are, the more applicable its principles are to the other sciences. Thus the principles of mathematics are applicable to natural things, but not vice versa, because physics presupposes mathematics; but the converse is not true, as is clear in the *De Caelo et Mundo.*[25]

So there are three levels of sciences concerning natural and mathematical entities. Some are purely natural and treat of the properties of natural things as such, like physics, agriculture, and the like. Others are purely mathematical and treat of quantities absolutely, as geometry considers magnitude and arithmetic number. Still

---

[23] For the meaning of "science of the moved sphere," see above, note 4.

[24] *Astrologia.* St. Thomas uses this term as synonymous with *astronomia,* one of the liberal arts. (See R. Deferrari, et al., *A Lexicon of St. Thomas Aquinas,* Fas. I, p. 93.) It has been translated *astronomy* throughout this work. St. Thomas defines it as "one of the mathematical sciences, whose subject is the heavens and celestial bodies." (*In III Meta.* lect. 7, n. 411.) However, he did not distinguish it from astrology, some of whose basic views he shared. For him, as for the mediaevals in general, the stars have an important influence on the sublunar world, and from a study of them at least some future events can be foreknown. But he excludes from their number all purely contingent and accidental events, both in human affairs and in natural happenings. See *Summa Theol.* 2-2.95.5; *De Judiciis Astrorum*; *De Occultis Operibus Naturae.* See also P. Choisnard, *Saint Thomas d'Aquin et l'influence des astres*; L. Thorndike, *A History of Magic and Experimental Science,* 2: 608-615; Pierre Duhem, *Le système du monde,* 3: 348-356; J. de Tonquédec, *Questions de cosmologie et de physique chez Aristote et saint Thomas,* pp. 16-68; J. McAllister, trans., *The Letter of St. Thomas Aquinas De Occultis Operibus Naturae,* pp. 150-155, 159-185; Th. Litt, *Les corps célestes dans l'univers de saint Thomas d'Aquin.*

[25] Aristotle, *De Caelo et Mundo* 3.1, 299a13-17.

others are intermediate,[26] and these apply mathematical principles to natural things; for instance, music, astronomy, and the like. These sciences, however, have a closer affinity to mathematics, because in their thinking that which is physical is, as it were, material, whereas that which is mathematical is, as it were, formal. For example, music considers sounds, not inasmuch as they are sounds, but inasmuch as they are proportionable according to numbers; and the same holds in other sciences. Thus they demonstrate their conclusions concerning natural things, but by means of mathematics. Therefore nothing prevents their being concerned with sensible matter insofar as they have something in common with natural science, but insofar as they have something in common with mathematics they are abstract.

Reply to 7. Because the intermediate sciences mentioned above have something in common with natural science as regards what is material in their procedure, but differ from it as regards what is formal in it, nothing prevents these sciences from occasionally having the same conclusions as natural science. Nevertheless, they do not use the same means of demonstration, unless the sciences are mixed and one occasionally uses what belongs to another, as the natural scientist proves that the earth is round from the movement of heavy bodies, while the astronomer proves it by considering eclipses of the moon.[27]

Reply to 8. As the Commentator says,[28] the Philosopher there did not intend to distinguish between the speculative sciences, because the natural scientist treats of everything subject to motion,

---

[26] See above, note 22.

[27] St. Thomas makes the same point in his *Summa Theologiae* 1.1.1, ad 2ᵐ, when distinguishing between the theology of Sacred Scripture and philosophy. For the proofs of the sphericity of the earth, see St. Thomas, *In II De Caelo et Mundo*, lect. 27-28.

[28] Averroes, *In II Phys.* 2, t. c. 71, fol. 74D-E.

whether it be corruptible or incorruptible, while the mathematician as such does not treat of anything subject to motion. But he intended to distinguish between the things studied by the speculative sciences, which must be treated separately and in order, although these three sorts of things can be apportioned to the three sciences. For incorruptible and immobile beings pertain precisely to the metaphysician. However, mobile and incorruptible beings, owing to their uniformity and regularity, can be determined in their movements by mathematical principles; this cannot be said of beings that are mobile and corruptible. Therefore, as Ptolemy says,[29] the second kind of beings is ascribed to mathematics through astronomy, while the third kind remains the proper domain of natural science alone.

ARTICLE FOUR

Does Divine Science Treat of What Exists Without Matter and Motion?

We proceed as follows to the fourth article:

It seems that divine science does not treat of things separate from motion and matter, for

1. Divine science seems to be especially concerned with God. Now we can come to know God only by way of his visible effects, which are created in matter and motion, as it is said in the Epistle to the Romans:[1] "The invisible things of him, from the creation of the world, are clearly seen, being understood by the things that are

[29] See above, note 6.

[1] Paul, Romans 1:20.

made." Therefore, divine science does not abstract from matter and motion.

2. Again, that to which motion in some way belongs is not entirely separate from motion and matter. But motion in some way belongs to God. Thus it is said in Wisdom[2] that the Spirit of Wisdom is "mobile" and "more mobile than all mobile things." And Augustine says[3] that God moves himself without time and place. Plato also asserted[4] that the First Mover moves itself. Therefore divine science, which treats of God, is not entirely separate from motion.

3. Again, divine science must treat not only of God but also of angels. But angels change both with regard to choice, because they became bad after having been good, and also with regard to place, as is evident in the case of those who are sent as messengers. So the objects of divine science are not entirely separated from motion.

4. Again, as the Commentator seems to say in the beginning of the *Physics*,[5] every being is either pure matter, or pure form, or a composite of matter and form. But an angel is not a pure form, because then he would be pure act, which is true of God alone. Neither is he pure matter. So he is a composite of matter and form. Therefore divine science does not abstract from matter.

5. Again, divine science, the third part of speculative philosophy, is the same as metaphysics, whose subject is being, and especially substantial being. This is clear in the *Metaphysics*.[6] But

[2] Wisdom 7:22, 24. "Mobile" here has the meaning of "active." The Douay translation runs: "For in her [i.e., Wisdom] is the spirit of understanding ... active... For Wisdom is more active than all active things."

[3] St. Augustine, *De Genesi ad Litteram* 8, n. 20 (CSEL 28: 259).

[4] See Aristotle, *Metaphysics* 12.6, 1072a1; Plato, *Phaedrus* 245C, *Timaeus* 30A, 34B.

[5] Averroes, *In I Phys.* 1, t. c. 1, fol. 6E.

[6] Aristotle, *Metaphysics* 4.1, 1003a21; 4.2, 1003b17.

being and substance do not abstract from matter; otherwise there would be no material being. So divine science does not abstract from matter.

6.   Again, according to the Philosopher,[7] it is the business of a science to consider not only a subject but also the divisions and attributes of that subject. Now, as we have said, being is the subject of divine science. Therefore it is the business of this science to treat of all beings. But matter and motion are beings. Therefore they come under the consideration of metaphysics, and so divine science does not abstract from them.

7.   Again, divine science demonstrates by means of three causes: efficient, formal, and final, as the Commentator says.[8] But we cannot consider an efficient cause without taking motion into account; and the same thing is true of a final cause, as the *Metaphysics* says.[9] Thus, because the objects of mathematics are immobile, there are no demonstrations through these causes in that science. Consequently, divine science does not abstract from motion.

8.   Again, in theology we treat of the creation of the heavens and the earth, of acts of men, and many similar things that involve matter and motion. So theology does not seem to abstract from matter and motion.

On the contrary, the Philosopher says in the *Metaphysics*[10] that "first philosophy deals with things that can exist separately," that is, from matter, "and with immobile things." Now first philosophy is divine science, as he says in the same place. Therefore divine science abstracts from matter and motion.

[7] Aristotle, *Posterior Analytics* 1.7, 75a39-b2; 1.10, 76b11-16.
[8] Averroes, *In I Phys.* 1, t. c. 1, fol. 6BC.
[9] Aristotle, *Metaphysics* 3.2, 996a22-27.
[10] Aristotle, *Metaphysics* 6.1, 1026a15.

Moreover, the most excellent science deals with the most excellent beings. But the most excellent science is divine science. Therefore, since immaterial and immobile beings are the most excellent, divine science will treat of them.

Moreover, the Philosopher says in the beginning of the *Metaphysics*[11] that divine science concerns first principles and causes. Now these are immaterial and immobile. Therefore things of this sort are the objects of divine science.

Reply: In order to throw light on this question we must understand what science should be called divine science. We must realize indeed that if a science considers a subject-genus,[12] it must investigate the principles of that genus, since science is perfected only through knowledge of principles, as the Philosopher explains in the beginning of the *Physics*.[13] Now there are two kinds of principles. Some are complete natures in themselves and nevertheless they are the principles of other things, as the heavenly bodies are principles of lower bodies and simple bodies are principles of mixed bodies. In the sciences, therefore, we study them not only insofar as they are principles, but also insofar as they are certain things in themselves. And for this reason they are considered not only in the science of the beings of which they are the principles, but also in a separate science. Thus there is a branch of natural science treating of heavenly bodies distinct from that treating of lower bodies, and there is one treating of the elements distinct from that treating of mixed bodies. There are some principles, however, that are not complete natures in themselves, but only principles of natures, as unity is the principle of number, point the principle of line, and form and matter prin-

---

[11] Aristotle, *Metaphysics* 1.1, 981b28.
[12] For the meaning of the subject of science, see above, Introduction, p. 17.
[13] Aristotle, *Physics* 1.1, 184a12-14.

ciples of natural bodies. Principles of this sort, then, are investigated only in the science dealing with the things of which they are principles.

Now just as there are certain common principles of any particular genus extending to all the principles of that genus, so too all beings, inasmuch as they share in being, have certain principles that are the principles of all beings. And as Avicenna says,[14] these principles can be called common in two ways: first, by predication, as when I say that form is common to all forms because it is predicated of all; second, by causality, as we say that the sun, which is numerically one, is the principle of all things subject to generation. Now there are principles common to all beings not only in the first way (in this sense the Philosopher says[15] that all beings have proportionately the same principles), but also in the second way, so that there are certain beings, each numerically one, which are the principles of all things. Thus the principles of accidents are reducible to the principles of substance, and the principles of perishable substances are reducible to imperishable ones, with the result that all beings are reducible to certain principles in a definite graded order. And since the principle of the being of all things must be being in the highest degree, as the *Metaphysics* says,[16] these principles must be most perfect and therefore supremely in act, so that they have no potentiality whatsoever, or the least possible, because actuality is prior to, and more excellent than potentiality, as the *Metaphysics* says.[17] For this reason they must be free from matter, which is in potency, and free from motion, which is the actuality of that which exists in potency. Divine

[14] Avicenna, *Sufficientia* 1.2, fol. 14^{va}6-30.
[15] Aristotle, *Metaphysics* 12.4, 1070a31-33; 12.5, 1071a30-35.
[16] Aristotle, *Metaphysics* 2.1, 993b24-31. See St. Thomas, *Summa Theol.* 1.2.3.
[17] Aristotle, *Metaphysics* 9.8, 1049b5; 9.9, 1051a4.

beings are of this sort, "because if the divine exists anywhere, it exists especially in such a nature" (that is to say, in a nature that is immaterial and immutable), as is said in the *Metaphysics*.[18]

Accordingly, because these divine beings are the principles of all things and nevertheless they are complete natures in themselves, they can be studied in two ways: first, insofar as they are the common principles of all things, and second insofar as they are beings in their own right. But even though these first principles are most evident in themselves, our intellect regards them as the eye of an owl does the light of the sun, as the *Metaphysics* says.[19] We can reach them by the light of natural reason only to the extent that their effects reveal them to us. It was in this way that the philosophers came to know them, as is clear from the Epistle to the Romans:[20] "The invisible things of God ... are clearly seen, being understood by the things that are made." Philosophers, then, study these divine beings only insofar as they are the principles of all things. Consequently, they are the objects of the science that investigates what is common to all beings, which has for its subject being as being. The philosophers call this divine science.

There is, however, another way of knowing beings of this kind, not as their effects reveal them, but as they reveal themselves. The Apostle mentions this way in his First Epistle to the Corinthians:[21] "So the things also that are of God no man knoweth, but the Spirit of God. Now we have received not the spirit of this world, but the

---

[18] Aristotle, *Metaphysics* 6.1, 1026a20. By "divine beings" St. Thomas means not only God but also angels. For a discussion of metaphysics as the science of immaterial substances, see J. Collins, *The Thomistic Philosophy of the Angels*, pp. 1-15. See above, p. 7.

[19] Aristotle, *Metaphysics* 2.1, 993b9-11.

[20] Romans 1:20.

[21] 1 Cor. 2:11-12.

Spirit that is of God, that we may understand." And again,[22] "But to us God hath revealed them by his Spirit." In this way we consider divine beings as they subsist in themselves and not only inasmuch as they are the principles of things.

Accordingly, there are two kinds of theology or divine science. There is one that treats of divine things, not as the subject of the science but as the principles of the subject. This is the kind of theology pursued by the philosophers and that is also called metaphysics. There is another theology, however, that investigates divine things for their own sakes as the subject of the science. This is the theology taught in Sacred Scripture.[23] Both treat of beings that exist separate from matter and motion, but with a difference, for something can exist separate from matter and motion in two distinct ways: first, because by its nature the thing that is called separate in no way can exist in matter and motion, as God and the angels are said to be separate from matter and motion. Second, because by its nature it does not exist in matter and motion; but it can exist without them, though we sometimes find it with them. In this way being, substance, potency, and act are separate from matter and motion, because they do not depend on them for their existence, unlike the objects of mathematics, which can only exist in matter, though they

---

[22] Ibid., 2:10.

[23] For St. Thomas' doctrine of theology as the science of Sacred Scripture, see *In I Sent.* prologus, 1; *In Lib. Boethii de Trinitate* 2.1-4; *Contra Gentiles* 1.3-4; *Summa Theol.* 1.1. See also M.-D. Chenu, *La théologie comme science au xiiie siècle*; M. Grabmann, *Die theol. Erkenntnis- und Einleitungslehre des hl. Thomas von Aquin auf Grund seiner Schrift "In Boethium de Trinitate."* For St. Thomas' notion of theology, see also G. F. Van Ackeren, *Sacra Doctrina. The Subject of the First Question of the Summa Theologiae of St. Thomas Aquinas*; E. Gilson, *Elements of Christian Philosophy*, pp. 22-42; M.-D. Chenu, *Is Theology a Science?*; idem, *Toward Understanding Saint Thomas*; Y. Congar, *Thomas d'Aquin: Sa vision de théologie et de l'église*, pp. 157-194.

can be understood without sensible matter. Thus philosophical theology investigates beings separate in the second sense as its subjects, and beings separate in the first sense as the principles of its subject.[24] But the theology of Sacred Scripture treats of beings separate in the first sense as its subjects, though it concerns some items in matter and motion insofar as this is needed to throw light on divine things.

Replies to Opposing Arguments:

Reply to 1.   When something is incorporated into a science only to throw light on something else, it does not belong to the science essentially, but, in a way, incidentally, as some mathematics are incorporated into the natural sciences. In this way nothing prevents some things in matter and motion being in divine science.

Reply to 2.   We do not attribute motion to God properly, but by a kind of metaphor, and this in two ways: first, according as the operation of the intellect or will is improperly called motion; and in this way a person is said to move himself when he knows or loves himself. In this sense, as the Commentator says,[25] the statement of Plato is true, that the First Mover moves himself because he knows and loves himself. Second, according as the flowing forth of effects from their causes can be called a procession or motion of cause to effect insofar as the likeness of the cause is left in the effect itself; and so the cause, which previously existed in itself, afterward comes to be in the effect through its likeness. And in this way God, who has communicated his likeness to all creatures, in a certain respect is said to be moved by all of them or to go forward to all things. Dionysius

[24] See St. Thomas, *In Meta.* Prooemium, trans. below, Appendix 2.

[25] Averroes, *In VIII Phys.* 4, t. c. 40, fol. 380D-F. See Plato, *Phaedrus* 245D, *Laws* 10, 895B.

frequently uses this manner of speaking.[26] This also seems to be the meaning of the statement in Wisdom,[27] that "Wisdom is more mobile than all mobile things," and that "She reacheth from end to end mightily." However, this is not motion in the proper sense of the term, and so the argument does not follow.

Reply to 3. Divine science received through divine inspiration does not treat of the angels as its subject, but only as something incorporated into the science to throw light on its subject. For Sacred Scripture treats of the angels just as it does other creatures. In the divine science taught by the philosophers, however, the angels, which they call Intelligences, are considered from the same point of view as the First Cause or God, insofar as they are also secondary principles of things, at least through the movement of the spheres,[28] though the angels themselves are subject to no physical motion. Moreover, motion with respect to choice is reducible to the sense in which the act of the intellect or will is called motion, which is an improper sense of the term, motion being understood as operation. Further, when angels are said to move in place, their motion is not with reference to enclosure in place but with reference to the activity they exercise in this or that place, or with reference to some other relation they have to place, although that relation is absolutely equivocal to that which a localized body has to place. So

---

[26] Pseudo-Dionysius, *De Divinis Nominibus* 5, n. 9 (PG 3: 825A), n. 10 (825B); 9, n. 1 (909B), n. 3 (912A), n. 9 (916C).

[27] Wisdom 7:24, 8:1.

[28] According to St. Thomas, the heavenly bodies through their movements are the causes of the generation and corruption of terrestrial bodies, and the movement of the heavenly bodies is caused by angels. See *Contra Gentiles* 2.70, 3.23, 3.24; *De Spiritualibus Creaturis* 6, Eng. trans. pp. 73-82; *Summa Theol.* 1.70.3. See also J. de Tonquédec, *Questions de cosmologie et de physique chez Aristote et saint Thomas*, pp. 46ff.

it is clear that they do not move in the sense in which we say natural things move.[29]

Reply to 4. Act and potency are more common than matter and form. Therefore, even though we do not find the composition of form and matter in the angels we can still find potency and act in them. For matter and form are parts of a thing composed of matter and form; and so we find the composition of matter and form only in things with parts, one of which is related to the other as potency to act. Now what can be, can also not be; and so one part can be found with or without the other; and therefore, as the Commentator says,[30] we find the composition of matter and form only in those things that are by nature corruptible. Nor is the objection valid, that an accident may be eternally conserved in a subject, like shape in the heavens. For a heavenly body cannot exist without such a shape, since shape and all accidents in general follow upon substance as their cause. So a subject is related to its accidents not only as passive potency, but also in a way as an active power; and for this reason some accidents are naturally conserved forever in their subjects. But matter is not the cause of form in this way; and therefore all matter subject to form can cease to be subject to it, unless perhaps an extrinsic cause preserves it; thus we maintain that by the divine power even some bodies composed of contraries, like the bodies of those arisen from the dead, are incorruptible.

Now, since the essence of an angel is incorruptible by its nature, it is not composed of form and matter. But an angel does not exist of himself, and so he is potential to the being (*esse*) he receives from

[29] For St. Thomas' view on the movement of angels in place, see *Summa Theol.* 1.53.1-3.

[30] Averroes, *In I de Caelo*, t. c. 20, fol. 15c; *In VIII Meta.* 2, t. c. 4, fol. 211f; 6, t. c. 12, fol. 220r.

God. Consequently, the being (*esse*) received from God is related to his simple essence as act to potency. This is what is meant by saying that angels are composed of *what they are* (*quod est*) and *that by which they are* (*quo est*); being (*esse*) is understood as *that by which they are* and the angelic nature as *what they are*.[31] However, even if angels were composed of matter and form, they would not be composed of sensible matter, from which both the objects of mathematics must be abstracted and those of metaphysics must be separated.

Reply to 5.   We say that being and substance are separate from matter and motion not because it is of their nature to be without them, as it is of the nature of ass to be without reason, but because it is not of their nature to be in matter and motion, although sometimes they are in matter and motion, as animal abstracts from reason, although some animals are rational.

Reply to 6.   The metaphysician deals with individual beings too, not with regard to their special natures, in virtue of which they are special kinds of being, but insofar as they share the common character of being. And in this way matter and motion also fall under his consideration.

Reply to 7.   Action and passion do not belong to things as they exist in thought but as they exist in reality. Now since the mathematician deals with things that are abstract only in thought, insofar as they come under his consideration they cannot be the principle or the end of motion. So the mathematician does not demonstrate

---

[31] See St. Thomas, *De Ente et Essentia* 4, ed. Leonine, p. 377.159-166, Eng. trans. p. 58; *Contra Gentiles* 2.52; *De Spiritualibus Creaturis* 1, Eng. trans. pp. 15-29; *Summa Theol.* 1.50.2; *De Substantiis Separatis* 8, ed. Leonine, p. D55.164-187, Eng. trans. p. 79. For the history of this doctrine, see M.-D. Roland-Gosselin, *Le "De Ente et Essentia,"* pp. 185-199; J. Collins, *The Thomistic Philosophy of the Angels,* pp. 75-93.

by means of efficient and final causes. But the things the meta-physician deals with are separate, existing in reality, and these can be the principle and end of motion. So nothing prevents his demonstrating by means of efficient and final causes.

Reply to 8. Just as faith, which is in a way the habit of the principles of theology, has for its object the First Truth itself, and yet the articles of faith contain certain other things relating to creatures insofar as they have some connection with the First Truth, in the same way theology is primarily concerned with God as its subject, but it includes many things about creatures as his effects, or as being in some way related to him.

Question Six

The Methods of Speculative Science

The next question concerns the methods ascribed by Boethius to the speculative sciences.[1] There are four points of inquiry in this connection:

1. Must we proceed according to the mode of reason in natural science, according to the mode of learning in mathematics, and according to the mode of intellect in divine science?[2]
2. Should we entirely abandon the imagination in divine science?
3. Can our intellect behold the divine form itself?
4. Can our intellect behold the divine form by means of some speculative science?

---

[1] See Boethius, *De Trinitate* 2, above, pp. 3-4.

[2] In the Latin text the three speculative sciences are said to proceed respectively *rationabiliter, disciplinabiliter,* and *intellectualiter.* The terms are taken from Boethius, ibid. See M.-D. Chenu, "Notes de lexicographie philosophique médiévale: *Disciplina,*" p. 687.

In Vernon Bourke's translation, the procedures of the sciences are called the ratiocinative method, learning method, and method of intellection (*The Pocket Aquinas,* pp. 38-42). C. A. L. Mendoza and J. E. Bolzán offer, as Spanish translations, *raciocinativamente, axiomáticamente* and *intelectualmente;* see "Santo Tomás y los metodos de las ciencias especulativas," *Sapientia* 27 (1972), 37-50. The translation of *disciplinaliter* by "axiomatically" brings out some aspects of its meaning: the self-evidence of the principles of mathematics and its certitude, but it fails to convey the basic meaning of *disciplina* as learning.

ARTICLE ONE

Must We Proceed according to the Mode of Reason in Natural Science, according to the Mode of Learning in Mathematics, and according to the Mode of Intellect in Divine Science?

(a)

On the first point we proceed as follows: It seems that we must not proceed according to the mode of reason in natural science, for

1. Rational philosophy is contradistinguished from natural philosophy.[3] But it seems to belong properly to rational philosophy to proceed according to the mode of reason. So this method is not appropriately ascribed to natural philosophy.

2. Again, in the *Physics*[4] the Philosopher frequently distinguishes between the methods of arriving at rational conclusions and physical conclusions. Therefore it is not the special characteristic of natural science to proceed rationally.

3. Again, what is common to all the sciences should not be reserved to one. But every science proceeds by reasoning, advancing from effects to causes or from causes to effects or from certain signs. So this method should not be reserved to natural science.

4. Again, in the *Ethics*[5] the Philosopher distinguishes the reasoning part of the soul from the scientific part. But natural philo-

---

[3] Throughout the Question the term "natural philosophy" is used synonymously with "physics" and "natural science." See above, Introduction, p. xv.

[4] Aristotle, *Physics* 3.5, 204b4, 10. Aristotle here distinguishes between a dialectical argument based on general notions and principles, which leads to a probable conclusion and a truly scientific argument based on principles proper to physics, which leads to truth. See St. Thomas, *In III Phys.* lect. 8, n. 1 and 5.

[5] Aristotle, *Nicomachean Ethics* 6.1, 1139a12. Aristotle here distinguishes between the calculating or deliberative part of the soul and the scientific part. The former is concerned with knowledge of things that are variable and contingent, e.g., individual human acts, the latter with what is necessary and invariable.

sophy belongs to the scientific part. Therefore it is not appropriately said to proceed according to the mode of reason.

On the contrary, the *De Spiritu et Anima*[6] says that reason is concerned with the forms of bodies. Now it belongs most especially to natural philosophy to consider bodies. Therefore the rational method is appropriately attributed to it.

Moreover, Boethius says:[7] "When reason contemplates some universal nature, using neither imagination nor sense, it nevertheless comprehends imaginable and sensible things." Now it belongs to the natural philosopher alone to comprehend what is imaginable and sensible. Therefore the rational method is suitably attributed to natural philosophy.

(*b*)

In the second place, it seems inappropriate to say that mathematics proceeds according to the mode of learning, for

1. Learning seems to be nothing else than the receiving of knowledge.[8] But we receive scientific knowledge in all branches of philosophy, because all proceed by means of demonstration. So it is common to all parts of philosophy to proceed according to the mode of learning; and so this procedure should not be made exclusive to mathematics.

2. Again, the more certain something is, the easier it seems to learn it. But natural things seem to be more certain than mathematics because they are apprehended by the senses, from which all our

---

[6] *Liber de Spiritu et Anima* 11 (PL 40: 787).

[7] Boethius, *De Consolatione Philosophiae* 5, prosa 4 (CSEL 67: 118.10-12).

[8] *Disciplina*, from which the English "discipline" is derived, comes from the Latin *discere*, which means to learn. For an historical study of the term in connection with the sciences, see M.-D. Chenu, "Notes de lexicographie...."

knowledge takes its origin. Therefore this method belongs to the natural philosopher rather than to the mathematician.

3. Again, as the *Metaphysics* says,[9] in the sciences we begin at the point from which we learn more easily. But learning begins with logic, which must be mastered before mathematics and all the other sciences. Therefore it belongs to logic rather than to the other sciences to proceed according to the mode of learning.

4. Again, the methods of natural and divine science are taken from powers of the soul, namely from reason and intellect. Therefore in the same way the method of mathematics ought to be taken from some power of the soul. So it is not appropriate to say that its method is to proceed according to the mode of learning.

On the contrary, to proceed according to the mode of learning is to proceed by demonstration and with certitude. But as Ptolemy says,[10] "Mathematics alone, if one applies himself diligently to it, will give the inquirer after knowledge firm and unshaken certitude by demonstrations carried out with unquestionable methods." Therefore it is most characteristic of mathematics to proceed according to the mode of learning.

Moreover, this is evident from the Philosopher who, in several places in his works, calls the mathematical sciences disciplines.[11]

(c)

In the third place, it seems that it is not appropriate to divine science to proceed according to the mode of intellect, for

---

[9] Aristotle, *Metaphysics* 5.1, 1013a2-5.

[10] Claudius Ptolemaeus, *Syntaxis Mathematica* 1.1 (*Opera Omnia* 1.6, 17-20).

[11] Aristotle, *De Caelo et Mundo* 3.1, 299a4. The English word "mathematics" is derived from the Greek *mathema*, which means knowledge in general and mathematical knowledge in particular. The corresponding Latin word is *disciplina*. Hence the close association of *disciplina* with mathematics. See M.-D. Chenu, "Notes de lexicographie...."

1.   According to the Philosopher,[12] there is understanding (*intellectus*)[13] of principles, whereas there is science of conclusions. But principles alone are not considered in divine science; some conclusions are also considered. Therefore to proceed according to the mode of intellect is not appropriate to divine science.

2.   Again, we cannot proceed intellectually with regard to those things that transcend every intellect. But divine things transcend every intellect, as Dionysius[14] and the Philosopher[15] say. Therefore they cannot be dealt with intellectually.

3.   Again, Dionysius says[16] that angels have intellectual power inasmuch as they do not gather their divine knowledge from what is sensible and divided; but, as he adds,[17] this is beyond the power of the soul. Therefore, since the divine science that is now under discussion is a science belonging to the human soul, it appears that its proper method is not to proceed intellectually.

4.   Again, theology seems particularly concerned with the things of faith. But understanding (*intelligere*) is the goal of the things of faith. Thus it is said in Isaiah, according to another version,[18]

---

[12]   Aristotle, *Posterior Analytics* 1.2, 71b17-18; 20-22; 2.19, 100b10; *Nicomachean Ethics* 6.6, 1141a7; 6.12, 1143a36.

[13]   *Intellectus* is the intellectual virtue of the understanding of first principles. See St. Thomas, *Summa Theol.* 1-2.57.2.

[14]   Pseudo-Dionysius, *De Divinis Nominibus* 1, n. 5 (PG 3: 593A).

[15]   *Liber de Causis* 5, ed. Bardenhewer, p. 169. As was customary at the time, St. Thomas here attributes this work to Aristotle. Later, when writing his commentary on it, he recognized that it is a translation of an Arabian work, drawn largely from Proclus' *Elements of Theology.* St. Thomas seems to have been the first to recognize this. See St. Thomas, *Expositio super Librum de Causis*, 1, ed. Saffrey, p. 3.

[16]   Pseudo-Dionysius, *De Divinis Nominibus* 7, n. 2 (PG 3: 868B).

[17]   Pseudo-Dionysius, ibid. (868C).

[18]   Isaiah 7:9. This is the reading of the Septuagint, used by St. Augustine, for example, in his *De Doctrina Christiana* 2.12 (PL 34: 43).

"Unless you believe, you will not understand." So we should not say that proceeding intellectually about divine things is the method of theology but the goal.

On the contrary, the *De Spiritu et Anima* says[19] that intellect (*intellectus*) has for its object created spirits, while understanding (*intelligentia*) has for its object God himself. Now divine science is principally concerned with them. Therefore it seems proper to it to proceed intellectually.

Moreover, the method of a science must correspond to its subject matter. But divine things are intelligible in virtue of themselves. Therefore the method appropriate to divine science is to proceed intellectually.

Reply: To the first question (*a*) I reply that a method of proceeding in the sciences is called rational in three ways:

In one way, because of the principles from which we begin; for instance, when we proceed to prove something beginning with mental beings, like genus, species, opposite, and concepts of this sort, which the logicians study. In this sense a method will be called rational when in a science we use the propositions taught in logic; namely, when we use logic as having a teaching function in the other sciences.[20] But this method of proceeding cannot belong properly to

---

[19] *Liber de Spiritu et Anima* 11 (PL 40: 787).

[20] *Logica docens.* Distinguished from *logica utens.* As here presented these are two types of applied logic. *Logica docens* teaches the other sciences the meaning of logical terms, which they can use in their demonstrations. For example, the metaphysician can use the logical notions of genus and species to prove the distinction between essence and existence (see below, Q. 6, a. 3, note 22). However, when the philosopher uses this method he proceeds dialectically, and his conclusions are only probable. (See *In IV Meta.* lect. 4, n. 574; *In I Post Anal.* lect.

any particular science: it will fall into error unless it proceeds from its own proper principles. However, logic and metaphysics may properly and suitably use this method, because both are universal sciences and in a sense treat of the same subject.[21]

In a second way, a method is called rational because of the end that terminates the thinking process. For the ultimate end that rational inquiry ought to reach is the understanding of principles, in which we resolve our judgments. And when this takes place, it is not called a rational procedure or proof but a demonstration. Sometimes, however, rational inquiry cannot arrive at the ultimate end, but stops in the course of the investigation itself; that is to say, when several possible solutions still remain open to the investigator. This happens when we proceed by means of probable arguments,[22] which by their nature produce opinion or belief, but not science. In this

---

20, n. 5. See also J. Isaac, "La notion de dialectique chez saint Thomas," *Revue des sciences phil. et théol.* 34 [1950], 497-503.)

Logica utens, on the other hand, is the use other sciences make of the rules of probable reasoning, described for example in Aristotle's *Topics.*

Sometimes, however, *logica docens* means the demonstrative science of logic, or pure logic; *logica utens* is applied logic. See *In I Post. Anal.* lect. 20, n. 5; *In IV Meta.* lect. 4, nn. 576-577; John of St. Thomas, *Ars Logica* 2, Q. 1, a. 4, pp. 277-284; J. Maritain, *A Preface to Metaphysics,* pp. 41-42.

[21] The logician, like the metaphysician, studies all beings, so that their subject matter is co-extensive. However, he studies all beings in a different way from the metaphysician. What he properly studies is second intentions, which are beings produced by the intellect and as such exist only in it. But these logical beings are co-extensive with the beings of nature, because all natural things can fall under the consideration of the intellect. See St. Thomas, *In IV Meta.* lect. 4, nn. 573-574; *In I Post Anal.* lect. 20, n. 5; J. Maritain, *A Preface to Metaphysics,* pp. 38-40. For the meaning of second intentions, see below, note 33.

[22] For St. Thomas' doctrine of probability, see Th. Deman, "Notes de lexicographie philosophique médiévale: *Probabilis,*" *Revue des sciences phil. et théol.* 22 (1933), 260-290; P. Gardeil, "La 'certitude probable'," *Revue des sciences phil. et théol.* 5 (1911), 237-266, 441-485.

sense, *rational* method is opposed to *demonstrative* method. We can proceed by this rational method in all the sciences, preparing the way for necessary proofs by probable arguments. This is another use of logic in the demonstrative sciences; not indeed as having a teaching function, but as being an instrument.[23] In these two ways, then, a method is called rational from rational science; for, as the Commentator says,[24] in both of them logic (which is another name for rational science) is used in the demonstrative sciences.

In a third way, a method is called rational from the rational power, that is, inasmuch as in our procedure we follow the manner proper to the rational soul in knowing; and in this sense the rational method is proper to natural science. For in its procedures natural science keeps the characteristic method of the rational soul in two ways. First, in this respect, that just as the rational soul receives from sensible things (which are more knowable relatively to us) knowledge of intelligible things (which are more knowable in their nature), so natural science proceeds from what is better known to us and less knowable in its own nature. This is evident in the *Physics.*[25] Moreover, demonstration by means of a sign or an effect is used especially in natural science. Secondly, natural science uses a rational method in this respect, that it is characteristic of reason to move from one thing to another; and this method is observed particularly in natural science, where we go from the knowledge of one thing to the knowledge of another; for example, from the knowledge of an effect to the knowledge of its cause. And the procedure in natural science is not only a movement from one thing to another distinct from it in the mind and not in reality, as when

[23] *Logica utens.* See above, note 20.
[24] Averroes, *In I Phys.* c. 2, t. c. 35, fol. 23c.
[25] Aristotle, *Physics* 1.1, 184a16-21.

we go from the concept *animal* to the concept *man*. In the mathematical sciences we proceed only by means of what is of the essence of a thing, since they demonstrate only through a formal cause. In these sciences, therefore, we do not demonstrate something about one *thing* through another *thing*, but through the proper definition of that thing. It is true that some demonstrations about the circle are made by means of the triangle or vice versa, but this is only because the triangle is potentially in the circle and vice versa.[26] But in natural science, where demonstration takes place through extrinsic causes, something is proved of one thing through another thing entirely external to it. So the method of reason is particularly observed in natural science; and on this account natural science among all the others is most in conformity with the human intellect. Consequently, we say that natural science proceeds rationally, not because this is true of it alone, but because it is especially characteristic of it.

Replies to Opposing Arguments:

Reply to 1. That argument is based on the method that is called rational in the first way. In this sense a rational method is proper to rational and divine science, but not to natural science.

Reply to 2. That argument is based on the method that is called rational in the second way.

Reply to 3. The method of reason is observed in all the sciences insofar as they proceed from one item to another that is mentally

---

[26] One mathematical figure or number is said to be potentially contained in another analogously to the way in which something actual is contained in something potential; for example, as the carved statue is contained potentially in the wood from which it is carved. However, this use of the term "potential" in mathematics is purely metaphorical. See St. Thomas, *Summa Theol.* 1-2.72.4, ad 2ᵐ; *In V Meta.* lect. 14, n. 974; *In IX Meta.* lect. 1, n. 1774.

distinct from it, but not in the sense that they go from one *thing* to another *thing*. As has been said, that is proper to natural science.

Reply to 4. In that place[27] the Philosopher considers the reasoning and deliberative parts of the soul to be identical: so it is clear that they are related to the second mode of rational procedure mentioned above. In the same place,[28] moreover, because of their contingency he assigns human actions, which are the objects of moral science, to the reasoning or deliberative part of the soul.

From what has been said, then, we can gather that the first mode of rationality is most characteristic of rational science, the second of moral science, and the third of natural science.

To the second question (*b*) I reply that mathematical science is said to proceed according to the mode of learning, not because it alone does so, but because this is especially characteristic of it. For, since learning is nothing else than the taking of knowledge from another, we are said to proceed according to the mode of learning when our procedure leads to certain knowledge, which is called science. Now this occurs particularly in the mathematical sciences. Because mathematics is situated between natural and divine science, it is more certain than either.[29] It is more certain than natural science because its investigation is not bound up with motion and matter, while the investigation of natural science centers upon matter and motion. Now from the very fact that natural science deals with matter, its knowledge depends upon many factors: upon the consideration of matter itself, of form, and of the material dispositions and properties accompanying form in matter. And whenever there are many factors to be considered in order to know something, know-

---

[27] Aristotle, *Nicomachean Ethics* 6.1, 1139a6-15.
[28] Aristotle, ibid.
[29] See St. Thomas, *In II Meta.* lect. 5, n. 336.

ledge is more difficult. Thus the *Posterior Analytics* says[30] that a science is less certain that results from adding on some item, as geometry adds something to arithmetic. If the inquiry in a science is about things that are mobile and lack uniformity, its knowledge is less exact because its demonstrations are often valid only in the majority of cases, owing to the fact that things sometimes happen differently. So, too, the more a science draws close to particulars (as do practical sciences like medicine, alchemy, and ethics), the less certain they can be because of the many factors to be taken into account in these sciences, the omission of any one of which will lead to error, and also because of their variability.

The method of mathematics is also more certain than the method of divine science, because the objects of divine science are further removed from sensible things, from which our knowledge takes its origin. This is true both in the case of the separate substances (to which our knowledge of the sense world gives us inadequate access), and also in the case of the principles common to all things (which are most universal and therefore furthest removed from the particular things falling under the senses). But mathematical entities do fall under the senses and they are objects of our imagination; for example, figures, lines, numbers, and the like. So the human intellect, which takes its knowledge from images, knows these things

[30] Aristotle, *Posterior Analytics* 1.27, 87a34-37. "... a science like arithmetic, which is constituted of fewer basic elements, is more exact than and prior to geometry, which requires additional elements. What I mean by 'additional elements' is this: a unit is substance without position, while a point is substance with position; the latter contains an additional element." From this point of view metaphysics is the most certain of the sciences, for it treats of being, while natural philosophy considers *mobile* being and mathematics *quantified* being. Thus the latter two sciences add something to the object of metaphysics. See St. Thomas, *In I Meta.* lect. 2, n. 47.

with greater ease and certainty than it does a separate Intelligence, or even the nature of substance, act, potency, and the like.

It is clear, then, that mathematical inquiry is easier and more certain than physical and theological, and much more so than that of the other sciences that are practical; and for this reason it is said especially to proceed according to the mode of learning. This is what Ptolemy asserts in the beginning of the *Almagest*.[31] "Let us call the other two kinds of theoretical knowledge opinion rather than science: theology because of its obscurity and incomprehensibility, physics because of the instability and obscurity of matter. The mathematical type of investigation alone will give the inquirer firm and unshaken certainty through demonstrations carried out by unquestionable methods."

Replies to Opposing Arguments:

Reply to 1. Although we learn in all the sciences, nevertheless, as we have said, we do so with greater ease and certitude in mathematics.

Reply to 2. Natural things come under the senses; but because of their instability when they begin to exist in reality they do not have the great certitude of the objects of mathematics. These latter are not subject to change; and yet they exist in sensible matter, and as such they can come under the senses and imagination.

Reply to 3. In learning we begin with what is easier, unless necessity dictates otherwise. For sometimes in learning it is necessary to start, not with what is easier, but with that on which the knowledge of subsequent matters depends. That is why in acquiring knowledge we must begin with logic;[32] not because it is easier than other sciences (for it involves the greatest difficulty, concerned as it

---

[31] Claudius Ptolemaeus, *Syntaxis Mathematica* 1.1 (*Opera Omnia* 1.6, 11-20).
[32] See below, Appendix 3.

is with second intentions),[33] but because the other sciences depend on it inasmuch as it teaches the method of proceeding in all the sciences. And, as the *Metaphysics* says,[34] we must know the method of science before science itself.

Reply to 4. The method of the sciences is taken from the powers of the soul because of the way in which these powers operate. So the methods of the sciences do not correspond to the soul's powers, but rather to the ways in which these powers can operate, and these are diversified not only according to the powers, but also according to their objects. So it is not necessary that the method of every science be named after a power of the soul. However, we can say that just as the method of physics is taken from reason inasmuch as it gets its objects from the senses, and the method of divine science is taken from the intellect inasmuch as it understands something purely and simply (*nude*),[35] so also the method of mathematics can be taken from reason inasmuch as it obtains its objects from the imagination.

To the third question (*c*) I reply that just as we attribute the rational method to natural philosophy because it adheres most closely to the method of reason, so we attribute the intellectual method to divine science because it adheres most closely to the method of intellect. Now reason differs from intellect as multitude

---

[33] These are the beings of the mind (for example, genus, species, difference) which are the subject matter of logic. First intentions are produced by the mind to represent directly real things (for example, man, tree); second intentions are produced by the intellect when it reflects upon its first intentions and their relations to each other. Hence they form part of the logical structure of knowing and cannot exist outside the intellect. See St. Thomas, *De Potentia*, 7, 9.

[34] Aristotle, *Metaphysics* 2.3, 995a12-14.

[35] Following the conjecture of P.-M. Gils that the correct reading of St. Thomas' text is *nude*, not *in Deo*. See *Bulletin Thomiste* 11 (1960-1961), 43. For St. Thomas' use of the expressions *nuda contemplatio* and *nude* see *Summa Theol.* 2-2.174, 2c and ad 1[m].

does from unity.[36] Thus Boethius says[37] that reasoning is related to understanding as time to eternity and as a circle to its center. For it is distinctive of reason to disperse itself in the consideration of many things, and then to gather one simple truth from them. Thus Dionysius says:[38] "Souls have the power of reasoning in that they approach the truth of things from various angles, and in this respect they are inferior to the angels; but inasmuch as they gather a multiplicity into unity they are in a way equal to the angels." Conversely, intellect first contemplates a truth one and undivided and in that truth comprehends a whole multitude, as God, by knowing his essence, knows all things. Thus Dionysius says:[39] "Angelic minds have the power of intellect in that they understand divine truths in a unified way."

It is clear, then, that rational thinking ends in intellectual thinking, following the process of analysis, in which reason gathers one simple *analysis* truth from many things. And again, intellectual thinking is the beginning of rational thinking, following the process of synthesis, in which the intellect comprehends a multiplicity in unity.[40] So the

[36] Reason and intellect are not distinct powers of the soul; they are distinct acts of the same power. The act of intellect is "to apprehend intelligible truth simply"; the act of reason is "to advance from one thing understood to another, so as to know an intelligible truth. ... Reasoning, therefore, is compared to understanding (*intelligere*) as movement is to rest, or acquisition to possession." St. Thomas, *Summa Theol.* 1.79.8. Hence the act of intellect or understanding is a simple intuition (*intuitus*) or grasping of an intelligible object present to the intellect. See St. Thomas, *In I Sent.* d. 3, q. 4, a. 5; *Summa Theol.* 1.79.8. See also J. Peghaire, *Intellectus et Ratio selon S. Thomas d'Aquin.*

[37] Boethius, *De Consolatione Philosophiae* 4, prosa 6 (CSEL 67: 98, 4-7).

[38] Pseudo-Dionysius, *De Divinis Nominibus* 7, n. 2 (PG 3: 868BC).

[39] Pseudo-Dionysius, ibid.

[40] Reasoning begins with understanding and ends in it. For we begin to reason from principles that we understand, and at the end of the reasoning we understand

thinking that is the terminus of all human reasoning is supremely intellectual.

Now all rational thinking in all the sciences, following the way of analysis, terminates in the knowledge of divine science. For, as we have said, reason sometimes advances from one thing to another in the order of reality; for example, when a demonstration is made through external causes or effects: by synthesis when we go from causes to effects, by analysis when we proceed from effects to causes, for causes are more simple, unchangeable, and uniformly constant than their effects. Consequently, the ultimate end of analysis in this process is attainment of the highest and most simple causes, which are the separate substances.[41] At other times, however, reason advances from one item to another distinct in the mental order, as when we proceed according to intrinsic causes: by synthesis when we go from the most universal forms to the more particular ones, by analysis when we proceed conversely, because what is more universal is more simple. Now that which is most universal is common to all beings; and so the ultimate end of analysis in this process is the consideration of being and the properties of being as being. And, as we said above, these are the objects of divine science; namely, the

---

the conclusions arrived at from the principles. The movement of reason from principles to conclusions is called "the way of composition or discovery" (*via compositionis vel inventionis*); the movement of reason from conclusions to principles in which it resolves or verifies its conclusions, is called "the way of resolution" (*via resolutionis*). The former is a movement of synthesis, in which reason goes from cause to effect, from the universal to the particular, from the simple to the multiple. The latter is a movement of analysis, in which reason proceeds in the opposite direction. See St. Thomas, *Summa Theol.* 1.79.8; *De Veritate* 10.8, ad 10[m]; 14, 1; 15, 1; *In II Meta.* lect. 1, n. 278. See also L.-M. Régis, "Analyse et synthèse dans s. Thomas," *Studia Mediaevalia* (1948), 303-330.

[41] That is, God and the angels, substances separated from matter.

separate substances and that which is common to all beings. It is evident, therefore, that its thinking is supremely intellectual.

It also follows that divine science gives principles to all the other sciences, because intellectual thinking is the starting point of rational thinking; and for this reason it is called *first philosophy*. Nevertheless it is learned after physics and the other sciences, because intellectual thinking is the terminus of rational thinking. For this reason it is called *metaphysics*, as if to say *beyond physics*, for in the process of analysis it comes after physics.[42]

Replies to Opposing Arguments:

Reply to 1. We say that divine science proceeds intellectually not as though it makes no use of reason, moving forward from principles to conclusions, but because its reasoning most closely approaches intellectual consideration and its conclusions are closest to its principles.

Reply to 2. God is beyond the comprehension of every created intellect, but he is not beyond the uncreated intellect, since in knowing himself he comprehends himself. However, he is above the intellect of everyone here on earth as regards knowing *what he is*, but not as regards knowing *that he is*.[43] The blessed in heaven, however, also know *what he is*, because they see his essence. Nevertheless divine science is not only about God. It is concerned with other things as well, which are not beyond the human intellect even in its present state as regards knowing *what* they are.

Reply to 3. As we said above, human thought at its terminus in a way approaches angelic knowledge; not that it equals it, but bears a resemblance to it. So Dionysius says:[44] "Souls, by reducing

---

[42] See above, Q. 5, a. 1, note 20.
[43] See below, Q. 6, a. 3, pp. 82-87.
[44] Pseudo-Dionysius, *De Divinis Nominibus* 7, n. 2 (PG 3: 868C).

multitude to unity, are rightly considered the equal of the angelic intelligences, as far as this is proper and possible to souls."

Reply to 4.   The knowledge of faith also belongs in a special way to understanding (*intellectus*). For we do not possess the things of faith through the investigation of reason, but we hold them by simply receiving understanding. But we are said not to understand them because the intellect does not have a full knowledge of them. That indeed is promised to us as our reward.

ARTICLE TWO

Should We Entirely Abandon the Imagination in Divine Science?

We proceed as follows to the second article:

It seems that in divine science we must turn to[1] images, for

1.   Divine science was never more appropriately taught than in Sacred Scripture. But treating of the divine in Sacred Scripture we resort to images when divine things are described for us under sensible figures. Therefore in divine science we must turn to images.

2.   Again, we grasp divine things only by the intellect; and this is why, as we have said,[2] we must proceed intellectually when

---

[1]   *Deduci ad.* The expression, which plays a central role in this article and which defies exact translation, comes from Boethius, *De Trinitate* 2 (PL 64: 1250B). It has the technical meaning of the intellect's being brought or led to something in which its judgment is verified. The intellect is said "to be led to" the senses, imagination, or the intellect itself, in the sense that it terminates its knowledge there, finding in the data grasped by the faculty in question the evidence on which it bases the truth of its judgment. The intellect is "led to" or "goes to" something as the final court of appeal for its judgment. See below, *Reply*, pp. 76-79. See also J. Maritain, *The Degrees of Knowledge*, pp. 53-56; *The Philosophy of Nature*, p. 25.

[2]   See above, Q. 6, a. 1, pp. 70-73.

treating of them. But, as the Philosopher says,[3] it is impossible to understand without the imagination. Therefore in divine science we must resort to images.

3. Again, we know the divine especially through divine illumination. But as Dionysius says:[4] "It is impossible for the divine light to illumine us from above unless it be hidden within the covering of many sacred veils." And he calls these sacred veils "images of sensible things."[5] So in divine science we must turn to images.

4. Again, when dealing with what is sensible we must make use of the imagination. But we know divine things from sensible effects, according to the statement of the Epistle to the Romans:[6] "The invisible things of God... are clearly seen, being understood by the things that are made." Therefore in divine science we must resort to images.

5. Again, in cognitive matters we are guided especially by the starting point of knowledge; for instance in the sciences of nature we are guided by the senses, from which our knowledge begins. Now in us intellectual knowledge begins in the imagination, since images are related to our intellect as colors to sight, as the De Anima says.[7] Therefore in divine science we must go to the imagination.

6. Again, since the intellect does not use a bodily organ, an injury to such an organ hinders the action of the intellect only insofar as it turns to the imagination. Now the intellect is hindered in its consideration of divine things through an injury of a bodily organ, namely the brain. Therefore in considering divine things the intellect resorts to the imagination.

---

[3] Aristotle, *De Anima* 1.1, 403a8; 3.7, 431a16.

[4] Pseudo-Dionysius, *De Caelesti Hierarchia* 1, n. 2 (PG 3: 121B).

[5] Pseudo-Dionysius, ibid. 1, n. 3 (PG 3: 124A).

[6] Romans 1:20.

[7] Aristotle, *De Anima* 3.7, 431a14.

On the contrary, Dionysius says in his *Mystical Theology*,[8] speaking to Timothy: "O beloved Timothy, in mystic contemplation abandon the senses." But the imagination has to do only with the sensible, for it is a movement produced by the sense in act, as the *De Anima* says.[9] Therefore, since the considerations of divine things are eminently mystical, we should not have recourse to images in them.

Moreover, in the procedure of any science we should avoid what leads to error in it. But, as Augustine says,[10] the principal error regarding divine things is the mistake of those who try to transfer to them what they know of the corporeal world. Therefore, since the imagination has to do only with the corporeal, it seems that in divine science we should not go to images.

Moreover, as is clear from Boethius,[11] a lower power does not extend to that which is proper to a higher power. But it belongs to an intellect and to an intelligence to know the divine and the spiritual, as is said in the *De Spiritu et Anima*.[12] Therefore, since, as is said in the same work,[13] imagination is below intelligence and intellect, it seems that in the domain of the divine and the spiritual we should not go to the imagination.

Reply: In all knowledge two factors must be taken into account: the beginning and the end. Knowledge begins with apprehension but it ends with judgment, for it is there that knowledge is completed.[14]

---

8 Pseudo-Dionysius, *De Mystica Theologia* 1, n. 1 (PG 3: 997B).

9 Aristotle, *De Anima* 3.3, 429a1.

10 St. Augustine, *De Trinitate* 1.1 (PL 42: 819).

11 Boethius, *De Consolatione Philosophiae* 5, prosa 4 (CSEL 67: 117, 29 - 118, 1).

12 *Liber de Spiritu et Anima* 11 (PL 40: 787).

13 Ibid. (PL 40: 786).

14 See above, Q. 5, a. 3, p. 35.

Now all our knowledge begins in the senses; from sense perception results the apprehension of the imagination (which is a movement arising from sensory knowledge, as the Philosopher says[15]), and from it in turn springs our intellectual apprehension, for images are like objects to the intellectual soul, as is clear in the *De Anima*.[16]

But knowledge does not always terminate in the same way. Sometimes it terminates in the senses, sometimes in the imagination, and sometimes in the intellect alone. In some cases the properties and accidents of a thing disclosed by the senses adequately reveal its nature,[17] and then the intellect's judgment of that nature must conform to what the senses reveal about it. All natural things, which are bound up with sensible matter, are of this kind. So the terminus of knowledge in natural science must be in the senses, with the result that we judge of natural beings as the senses manifest them, as is evident in the *De Caelo et Mundo*.[18] Accordingly, the man who neglects the senses when dealing with natural things falls into error. By natural things I mean those that are bound up with sensible matter and motion both in existence and in thought.

Our judgment about some things, however, does not depend upon what the sense perceives, because even though they exist in sensible matter they abstract from it when their essences are defined; and we judge of anything chiefly according to the definition of its essence.

---

[15] Aristotle, *De Anima* 3.3, 429a1.

[16] Aristotle, *De Anima* 3.7, 431a14.

[17] On the other hand, St. Thomas says that sometimes the essential differences of things are unknown to us. In these cases we must use accidental characteristics and empiriological signs in place of essential properties in order to know things. See St. Thomas, *De Veritate* 4.1, ad 8[m]; 10.1 and ad 6[m]; *Contra Gentiles* 1.3; *In VII Meta.* lect. 12, n. 1552. See also J. Maritain, *The Degrees of Knowledge*, pp. 176-177, 204-205, 207.

[18] Aristotle, *De Caelo et Mundo* 3.7, 306a16.

But because they do not abstract from every kind of matter when their essences are defined but only from sensible matter, and because an object for the imagination remains after sensible characteristics have been set aside, we must judge about such things according to what the imagination reveals. Now the objects of mathematics are of this kind. Accordingly, the knowledge we have through judgment in mathematics must terminate in the imagination and not in the senses, because mathematical judgment goes beyond sensory perception. Thus, the judgment about a mathematical line is not always the same as that about a sensible line. For example, that a straight line touches a sphere at only one point is true of an abstract straight line but not of a straight line in matter, as is said in the *De Anima*.[19]

There are other beings, however, that transcend both that which falls under the senses and that which falls under the imagination; namely, those that are entirely independent of matter both with respect to their being and with respect to their being understood. So, when we know things of this kind through judgment, our knowledge must terminate neither in the imagination nor in the senses. Nevertheless we reach some knowledge of them through the objects of the senses and the imagination, either by way of causality (as when from an effect we come to know its cause, which is not proportionate to the effect but transcends it), or by way of transcendence, or by way of negation (as when we separate from such beings whatever the sense or imagination apprehends). These are the means of knowing divine things from the sensible world proposed by Dionysius in his *Divine Names*.[20]

It follows that we can use the senses and the imagination as the starting points but not as the termini of our knowledge of divine

---

[19]   Aristotle, *De Anima* 1.1, 403a13-16.
[20]   Pseudo-Dionysius, *De Divinis Nominibus* 7, n. 3 (PG 3: 869C-872A).

things, so that we judge them to be the sort of objects the sense or the imagination apprehends. Now to go to something is to terminate at it.[21] Therefore, we should go neither to the imagination nor to the senses in divine science, to the imagination and not to the senses in mathematics, and to the senses in the natural sciences. For this reason they are in error who try to proceed in the same way in these three parts of speculative science.

Replies to Opposing Arguments:

Reply to 1.   Sacred Scripture does not present divine things to us under sensible images so that our intellect may stop with them, but that it may rise from them to the immaterial world. Thus, as Dionysius says,[22] it even teaches the divine through symbols of base objects in order to offer less occasion of stopping with them.

Reply to 2.   The operation of our intellect in its present state is never without an image as regards the beginning of knowledge. But our knowledge need not always terminate at images, so that, in other words, we judge the objects of our understanding to be of the same kind as the objects of the imagination.

Reply to 3.   The text of Dionysius refers to the beginning of knowledge and not to its end, which is reached when we know divine things from their sensible effects by the three methods described above; but not in such a way that we must form our judgment of the divine according to the manner of being of these sensible effects.

Reply to 4.   That argument is valid when the starting point of knowledge adequately leads to the object we seek to know. This is the way the senses are the starting point in the natural sciences, but not, as we have said, in divine science.

---

[21] See above, note 1.
[22] Pseudo-Dionysius, *De Caelesti Hierarchia* 2, n. 2 (PG 3: 140A).

Reply to 5. An image is the starting point of our knowledge, for it is that from which the operation of the intellect begins; not that it passes away, but it remains as the foundation of intellectual activity, just as the principles of demonstration must remain throughout the whole process of science. This is because images are related to the intellect as objects in which it sees whatever it sees, either through a perfect representation or through a negation. Consequently, when our knowledge of images is impeded, we must be completely incapable of knowing anything with our intellect even about divine things. Clearly, we cannot know that God causes bodies, or transcends all bodies, or is not a body, if we do not form an image of bodies; but our judgment of what is divine is not made according to the imagination. Consequently, even though in our present state of life the imagination is necessary in all our knowledge of the divine, with regard to such matters we must never terminate in it.[23]

ARTICLE THREE

Can Our Intellect Behold the Divine Form Itself?

We proceed as follows to the third article:

It seems that we are unable to behold the divine form itself, at least in this life, for

1. As Dionysius says,[1] "If anyone seeing God understood what he saw, he did not see God himself but one of his creations." Now the divine form is God himself. Therefore we are not able to behold the divine form itself.

---

[23] The reply to 6 is contained in the reply to 5.

[1] Pseudo-Dionysius, *Epistola* 1 (PG 3: 1065A).

2. Again, the divine form is the divine essence itself. Now no one in the present life can see God through his essence. Therefore neither can he behold the divine form.

3. Again, if we see the form of something, we have some knowledge of that thing. But according to Dionysius,[2] our intellect is most united to God when it knows absolutely nothing of him. Therefore we are unable to behold the divine form.

4. Again, as was said above,[3] all our knowledge begins from the senses. But what we perceive by the senses is inadequate to reveal the divine form or even the other separate substances. Therefore we are unable to behold the divine form itself.

5. Again, according to the Philosopher,[4] our intellect is related to what is most evident as the eye of an owl to the sun. But the eye of an owl cannot see the sun at all. Therefore neither can our intellect see the divine form itself or other separate forms, which are nature's most evident beings.

On the contrary, the Apostle says in the Epistle to the Romans:[5] "The invisible things of God are clearly seen by a creature of the world" (that is, by man), "... his eternal power also and divinity." Now the divine form is simply the divinity itself. Therefore in some way we can know the divine form with our intellect.

Moreover, commenting on the text of Genesis,[6] "I have seen God face to face," the gloss of Gregory says:[7] "Unless a person somehow

[2] Pseudo-Dionysius, *De Mystica Theologia* 1, n. 3 (PG 3: 1001A).

[3] See above, Q. 6, a. 2, p. 77.

[4] Aristotle, *Metaphysics* 2.1, 993b9-11.

[5] Romans 1: 20. Here St. Thomas interprets *a creatura mundi* to mean "by a creature of the world," namely man. He also gives the more common interpretation of the expression ("from the creation of the world") in his Commentary on the Epistle to the Romans 1, lect. 6.

[6] Genesis 32:30.

[7] Paterius, *Liber de Expositione V. ac N. Testamenti*, compiled from various

beheld it" (namely, divine truth), "he would not feel himself incapable of beholding it." But we feel that we cannot perfectly see the divine essence. Therefore in some way we do behold it.

Moreover, Dionysius says[8] that "the human mind gradually becomes accustomed to rise from the world of sense to heights beyond this world," which are nothing else than the separate forms.[9] Therefore we can somehow know the separate forms.

Reply: We know a thing in two ways: in one way when we know *that it is*, and in another way when we know *what it is.*[10] Now in order to know *what* anything is, our intellect must penetrate its quiddity or essence either directly or by means of other things that adequately

---

works of St. Gregory the Great, pars 1, lib. 1, c. 48 (PL 79: 717c); see St. Gregory, *Moralia* 24.6 (PL 76: 292c).

   [8] Pseudo-Dionysius, *De Caelesti Hierarchia* 2, n. 5 (PG 3: 164A).

   [9] That is, God and the angels, spiritual beings separate from matter.

   [10] This is the distinction between knowing the answer to the question "whether a thing is" (*an est*) and the answer to the question "what a thing is" (*quid est*). See Aristotle, *Posterior Analytics* 2.7, 92b11ff. In the precise sense of the term, to know of anything *quid est* we must grasp its essence in itself, so as to be able to define it by its essential properties and to give the reason for those properties and for the very existence of the thing. It is in this sense of the term that St. Thomas denies that we can know the *quid est* of God in this life. He says, "With regard to God, *quid est* remains wholly unknown." The Blessed in heaven, however, see the essence of God in itself, without the intermediary of any created likeness or representation. Here on earth we can know the essence of God only as it is represented by creatures, and therefore we cannot know of it *quid est*. See St. Thomas, *Contra Gentiles* 1.30, 3.49; *In Boethium de Trinitate*, Q. 1, a. 2; *In II Post. Anal.* lect. 1, n. 8. For discussions of this doctrine, see J. Maritain, *The Degrees of Knowledge*, pp. 422-429; E. Gilson, *The Christian Philosophy of St. Thomas Aquinas*, pp. 103-110; J. Anderson, *The Bond of Being*, p. 266 and note 13; H. F. Dondaine, "Cognoscere de Deo 'quid est'," *Recherches de théol. ancienne et médiévale* 22 (1955), 72-78; A. C. Pegis, "Penitus Manet Ignotum," *Mediaeval Studies* 27 (1965), 212-226; J. F. Wippel, "Quidditative Knowledge of God," in *Metaphysical Themes in Thomas Aquinas*, pp. 215-241.

reveal its quiddity. But in this life our intellect cannot directly penetrate the essence of God or other separate essences,[11] because it directly extends to images, to which it bears the same relation as sight does to color, as the *De Anima* says.[12] So the intellect can directly conceive the quiddity of a sensible reality but not of an intelligible reality. Thus Dionysius says:[13] "According to our way of knowing, we cannot immediately attain to the contemplation of the invisible." There are some invisible things, however, whose quiddity or nature is perfectly revealed by the known quiddities of sensible things; and we can also know what these intelligible objects are, although indirectly. For instance, from the fact that we know what man and animal are, we come to know adequately the relation of one to the other, and from this we know what a genus and a species are.[14] But the sensible natures known to us do not adequately reveal the divine essence or even other separate essences, since naturally considered they do not belong to one genus;[15] and *quiddity* and all

---

[11] That is, angels.

[12] Aristotle, *De Anima* 3.7, 431a14.

[13] Pseudo-Dionysius, *De Caelesti Hierarchia* 2, n. 2 (PG 3: 140A).

[14] Both genus and species designate relations: genus the relation of an essence to many things different in species (for example, animal to rational and irrational animal); species the relation of an essence to many things different in number (for example, man to Peter, Paul, etc.). For St. Thomas' doctrine of genus and species and their relation to the essences of things, see his *De Ente et Essentia* 3, ed. Leonine, pp. 374-375; Eng. trans. pp. 45-50.

[15] From the point of view of the logician, material and immaterial things can be brought under the same logical genus (for example, substance), because he considers them only as concepts in the mind. From the point of view of the natural philosopher or metaphysician, however, they do not come under the same genus because these philosophers consider the natures of things as they actually exist in reality, and in actual existence the substance of material things is not the same as that of immaterial things. Hence from a logical point of view, the genus of substance is predicated univocally of all substances; but from the point of view of the natural philosopher and the metaphysician it is predicated analogically. For this distinction

such terms are predicated almost equivocally[16] of sensible things and of these substances. That is why Dionysius calls[17] the likenesses of sensible things, transferred to immaterial substances, "unlike likenesses, which intellectual beings participate in one way and sensible beings in another." Consequently, we cannot have adequate knowledge of the former from the latter by way of likeness or even by way of causality, because the effects of those substances found in lower beings do not measure up to their powers so that we can come to know the essence of their cause in this way.

Accordingly, in the present life it is absolutely impossible to know the essence of immaterial substances, not only by natural knowledge but also by revelation; for, as Dionysius says,[18] the light of divine revelation comes to us adapted to our condition. Thus even though revelation elevates us to know something of which we should otherwise be ignorant, it does not elevate us to know in any other way than through sensible things. Thus Dionysius says:[19] "It is impossible for the divine light to illumine us from above unless it be hidden within the covering of many sacred veils." Now knowledge by way of the sensible is inadequate to enable us to know the essences of immaterial substances. So we conclude that we do not know *what* immaterial forms are, but only *that* they are, whether by

---

between logical and natural genus, see St. Thomas, *In I Sent.* d. 19, q. 5, a. 2, ad 1ᵐ; *In X Meta.* lect. 12, nn. 2142-2144; *Summa Theol.*, 1.66.2, ad 2ᵐ; 88.2, ad 4ᵐ.

[16] "Almost equivocally," or in other words, analogically. For St. Thomas' doctrine of analogy, see G. B. Phelan, *St. Thomas and Analogy*; J. Anderson, *The Bond of Being*; R. M. McInerny, *The Logic of Analogy*; J. Owens, "Analogy as a Thomistic Approach to Being," *Mediaeval Studies* 24 (1962), 303-322. For the analogical character of essence, see J. Maritain, "Sur la doctrine de l'aséité divine," *Mediaeval Studies* 5 (1943), 39-50.

[17] Pseudo-Dionysius, *De Caelesti Hierarchia* 2, n. 4 (PG 3: 141C).

[18] Pseudo-Dionysius, ibid., 1, n. 2 (PG 3: 121B).

[19] Pseudo-Dionysius, ibid.

natural reason based upon created effects or even by revelation, by means of likenesses taken from sensible things.

It should be noticed, however, that we cannot know *that* a thing is without knowing in some way *what* it is, either perfectly or at least confusedly, as the Philosopher says[20] we know things defined before we know the parts of their definition. For if a person knows that man exists and wants to find out what man is by definition, he must know the meaning of the term "man." And this is possible only if he somehow forms a concept of what he knows to exist, even though he does not know its definition. That is to say, he forms a concept of man by knowing a proximate or remote genus and accidental characteristics which reveal him externally. For our knowledge of definitions, like that of demonstrations, must begin with some previous knowledge.[21] Similarly, therefore, we cannot know *that* God and other immaterial substances exist unless we know somehow, in some confused way, *what* they are. Now we cannot do this by knowing a proximate or remote genus, for God is in no genus, since his essence is not distinct from his being: a condition required in all genera, as Avicenna says.[22] Created immaterial substances, however, are indeed in a genus; but even though from the viewpoint

---

[20] Aristotle, *Physics* 1.1, 184a23-b14: "Now what is to us plain and obvious at first is rather confused masses, the elements and principles of which become known to us later by analysis. Thus we must advance from generalities to particulars ... a child begins by calling all men 'father,' and all women 'mother,' but later on distinguishes each of them."

[21] For the necessity of precognition in our knowledge of definitions and demonstrations, see *In I Post. Anal.* lect. 1-3; *De Veritate* 1.1.

[22] Avicenna, *Metaphysics* 8.4, ed. Van Riet, 2: 402.61-403.73. See St. Thomas: "(God) is not in a genus, for everything in a genus must have a quiddity in addition to its being. The reason for this is that the quiddity or nature of a genus or species does not differ, as regards the notion of the nature, in the individuals in the genus or species, whereas being is diverse in these different individuals." *De Ente et Essentia* 5, ed. Leonine, p. 378.8-14; Eng. trans. p. 60.

of logic they share the same remote genus of substance with sensible substances, from the viewpoint of physics they do not belong to the same genus, as neither do heavenly and terrestrial bodies. For the corruptible and the incorruptible do not belong to the same genus, as the *Metaphysics* says.[23] For the logician considers concepts in themselves; and from this point of view nothing prevents the immaterial and the material, or the incorruptible and the corruptible, from having something in common. But the philosopher of nature and the metaphysician treat of essences as existing in reality; and therefore they say that there are different genera wherever they find diverse modes of potency and act, and consequently diverse modes of being. Neither has God any accidental characteristics, as we will prove later.[24] If other immaterial substances have such characteristics, we do not know them.

Accordingly, we cannot say that we know immaterial substances obscurely by knowing their genus and observable accidents. Instead of knowing the genus of these substances, we know them by negations; for example, by understanding that they are immaterial, incorporeal, without shapes, and so on. The more negations we know of them the less vaguely we understand them, for subsequent negations limit and determine a previous negation as differences do a remote genus.[25] Our knowledge of the heavenly bodies is also negative for the most part, because they belong to a different genus from that of inferior bodies. We know, for instance, that they are not light or heavy, or hot or cold.[26] And instead of accidental charac-

---

[23] Aristotle, *Metaphysics* 10.10, 1058b26-28, 1059a9. See above, note 15.

[24] St. Thomas did not discuss this question in the present work, which he left incomplete. On this point, see his *Contra Gentiles* 1.23; *Summa Theol.* 1.3.6.

[25] See St. Thomas, *Contra Gentiles* 1.14; E. Gilson, *The Christian Philosophy of St. Thomas Aquinas*, pp. 97-103.

[26] According to mediaeval astronomy, the heavenly bodies were not composed of the four elements of fire, air, water, and earth, but of a fifth type of matter or "fifth

teristics in these substances we have their connections with sensible ones, either with regard to the relationship of cause to effect or with regard to the relationship of transcendence.

We conclude, then, that in the case of immaterial forms we know *that* they exist; and instead of knowing *what* they are we have knowledge of them by way of negation, by way of causality, and by way of transcendence.[27] These are the same ways Dionysius proposes in his *Divine Names*;[28] and this is how Boethius[29] understands that we can know the divine form by removing all images, and not that we know *what* it is.

The solution of the opposing arguments is clear from what has been said; for the first arguments are based on perfect knowledge of what a thing is, the others on imperfect knowledge of the sort described.

---

essence" (*quinta essentia*). Hence they do not have the properties of being hot or cold, light or heavy, which belong to the four elements. On this point, see St. Thomas, *In I De Caelo et Mundo*, lect. 5, nn. 5-7; lect. 6. See also J. de Tonquédec, *Questions de cosmologie et de physique chez Aristote et saint Thomas*, pp. 17-21.

[27] "There is something with regard to God which is entirely unknown to man in this life, namely, what God is (*quid est Deus*)... And this is so because man's knowledge begins with the things that are connatural to him, namely, sensible creatures, which are not adequate to represent the divine essence. Nevertheless man can know God from creatures of this sort in three ways, as Dionysius says in the *Divine Names*. First, through causality. For, since such creatures are imperfect and changeable, they must be reduced to some unchangeable and perfect principle. And from this we know that God exists (*de Deo an est*). Second, by way of excellence (*per viam excellentiae*). For all things are reduced to a first principle, not as to a proper and univocal cause, as man begets man, but as to a universal and transcendent cause. And from this we know that he is above all things. Third, by way of negation, because if he is a transcendent cause, nothing which is in creatures can belong to him..." *In Epistolam ad Romanos* 1, lect. 6. See *Contra Gentiles* 1.30, 3.49.

[28] Pseudo-Dionysius, *De Divinis Nominibus* 7, n. 3 (PG 3: 869D-872A).

[29] Boethius, *De Trinitate* 2, above, p. 3.

ARTICLE FOUR

Can Our Intellect Behold the Divine Form by Means of Some Speculative Science?

We proceed as follows to the fourth article:

It seems that we can come to behold the divine form through the speculative sciences, for

1. As Boethius says here,[1] theology is a part of speculative science. But, as he says,[2] it belongs to theology to behold the divine form itself. Therefore we can arrive at a knowledge of that form through the speculative sciences.

2. Again, there is a speculative science treating of immaterial substances, namely divine science. Now any science treating of a substance beholds the form of that substance, because all knowledge is by means of form, and according to the Philosopher[3] all demonstration begins with essence. Therefore we can behold separate forms through the speculative sciences.

3. Again, according to the philosophers,[4] the ultimate happiness of man is to understand the separate substances. For, since happiness is the most perfect activity, it must have to do with the most excellent things falling under the intellect, as we can learn from the Philosopher in the *Ethics*.[5] Now the happiness described by the philosophers is an activity springing from wisdom, since wisdom is

---

[1] Boethius, *De Trinitate* 2, above, p. 3.

[2] Ibid.

[3] Aristotle, *Posterior Analytics* 2.3, 90b24; *Metaphysics* 7.9, 1034a31.

[4] See Aristotle, *Nicomachean Ethics* 10.7, 1177a19-21; Avicenna, *Liber de Anima*, ed. Van Riet, 2, pp. 147-151; Averroes, *In III De Anima*, t. c. 36, fol. 174ᵛ-187. On this point, see St. Thomas, *Contra Gentiles* 3.41-45; *Summa Theol.* 1.88.1-2.

[5] Aristotle, *Nicomachean Ethics* 10.7, 1177a12-21.

the most perfect virtue of the most perfect power—the intellect; and, as the *Ethics* says,[6] this activity is happiness. Through wisdom, therefore, we understand the separate substances. Now wisdom is a speculative science, as is clear in the *Metaphysics*[7] and *Ethics*.[8] So we can understand the separate substances through the speculative sciences.

4. Again, if something is unable to reach the end for which it exists it is to no purpose. But the inquiry in all the speculative sciences is directed to a knowledge of the separate substances as to its end, because in any class of things the most perfect is the goal [of all the rest]. Therefore if substances of this sort cannot be understood through the speculative sciences, all of them would be to no purpose, which is absurd.

5. Again, everything directed by nature to an end has been previously endowed with principles by which it is able to arrive at that end and by which it also tends toward that end; for the principles of natural motions are within a thing. Now the end of man to which he is directed by nature is to know the immaterial substances, as both the saints and the philosophers teach. So man is naturally endowed with principles of that knowledge. But everything we can arrive at from naturally known principles is included in one of the speculative sciences. Therefore the knowledge of immaterial substances pertains to some speculative sciences.

On the contrary, the Commentator says[9] that there are two possible consequences of this position. Either the speculative sciences are not yet perfect, because we have not discovered the

---

[6] Aristotle, ibid.
[7] Aristotle, *Metaphysics* 1.1, 981b28-982a3.
[8] Aristotle, *Nicomachean Ethics* 6.7, 1141a18-20, b2.
[9] Averroes, *In III De Anima*, t. c. 36, fol. 182E-183B.

sciences by which we can know the separate substances, and this owing to the fact we do not yet understand these substances because of our ignorance of some principles; or if it happens because of some defect in our nature that we cannot discover the speculative sciences by which these substances may be known, it follows that, if some men can discover these sciences, we and they are men only in an equivocal sense. The first of these is improbable; the second is impossible. So we cannot understand these substances through some speculative sciences.

Moreover, in the speculative sciences we search after definitions, by which we understand the essences of things through the division of a genus into differences and through the examination of a thing's causes and accidents, which contribute a great deal to our knowledge of the essence. But we cannot know these in the case of immaterial substances, because, as we have already said,[10] from the viewpoint of physics they have no genus in common with the sensible substances known to us. And either they do not have a cause, as in the case of God, or their cause is deeply hidden from us, as in the case of the angels. Their accidents are also unknown to us. So there can be no speculative science through which we may come to understand immaterial substances.

Moreover, in the speculative sciences we know the essences of things through definitions. Now a definition is a phrase made up of a genus and differences. But the essences of these substances are simple and there is no composition in their quiddities, as is clear from the Philosopher and the Commentator.[11] So we cannot understand these substances through the speculative sciences.

---

[10] See above, Q. 6, a. 3, p. 83.
[11] Aristotle, *Metaphysics* 9.10, 1051b27; Averroes, *In IX Meta.* t. c. 22, fol. 248D.

Reply: In the speculative sciences we always proceed from something previously known, both in demonstrating propositions and also in finding definitions. For just as one comes to know a conclusion by means of propositions previously known, so also from the concept of a genus and difference and from the causes of a thing he comes to know its species. But it is impossible to go on to infinity in this case, because then all science would cease, both as regards demonstrations and as regards definitions, since the infinite cannot be traversed. So inquiry in all the speculative sciences works back to something first given, which one does not have to learn or discover (otherwise he would have to go on to infinity), but which he knows naturally. Such are the indemonstrable principles of demonstration (for example, Every whole is greater than its part, and the like), to which all demonstrations in the sciences are reducible. Such, too, are the first conceptions of the intellect (for example, being, one, and the like), to which all definitions in the sciences must be reduced.

From this it is clear that the only things we can know in the speculative sciences, either through demonstration or definition, are those that lie within the range of these naturally known principles. Now these principles are revealed to man by the light of the agent intellect, which is something natural to him; and this light makes things known to us only to the extent that it renders images actually intelligible; for in this consists the operation of the agent intellect, as the *De Anima* says.[12] Now images are taken from the senses. So our knowledge of the above-mentioned principles begins in the senses and memory, as is evident from the Philosopher.[13] Conse-

---

[12] Aristotle, *De Anima* 3.5, 430a15. See St. Thomas, *Summa Theol.* 1.79.3, 1.85.1.

[13] Aristotle, *Posterior Analytics* 2.19, 100a3-9.

quently, these principles do not carry us beyond that which we can know from the objects grasped by the senses.[14]

Now we cannot know the essence of the separate substances through that which we take from the senses. This is clear from what was said above. But through sensible things we can arrive at a knowledge of the existence of these substances and of some of their characteristics. So we cannot know the quiddity of any separate substance by means of a speculative science, though the speculative sciences enable us to know the existence of these substances and some of their traits; for instance, that they are intellectual, incorruptible, and the like. This is also the teaching of the Commentator.[15] Avempace was of the opposite opinion;[16] he thought that the quiddities of sensible things adequately reveal immaterial quiddities; but, as the Commentator says,[17] this is clearly false, because quiddity is predicated of both almost in an equivocal sense.

Replies to Opposing Arguments:

Reply to 1.   Boethius does not intend to say that through the science of theology we can contemplate the essence of the divine form itself, but only that is transcends all images.

Reply to 2.   Some things are knowable to us through themselves; and in clarifying them the speculative sciences use the definitions of these objects to demonstrate their properties, as in the case of the sciences that demonstrate through causes.[18] Other things are not knowable to us through themselves but through their effects. If the

[14]   See St. Thomas, *Summa Theol.* 1-2.3.6.

[15]   Averroes, *In III De Anima*, t. c. 36, fol. 182BD.

[16]   St. Thomas knew Avempace's doctrine through Averroes, who refers to it in his Commentary on the *De Anima*, ibid., fol. 182DE. See *Contra Gentiles* 3.41.

[17]   Averroes, ibid. Essence or quiddity is predicated *quasi aequivoce* of God and creatures, that is, analogically. See above, Q. 6, a. 3, p. 84, and note 16.

[18]   See above, Q. 5, a. 1, note 48.

effect is proportionate to its cause, we take the quiddity itself of the effect as our starting point to prove that the cause exists and to investigate its quiddity, from which in turn its properties are demonstrated. But if the effect is not proportionate to its cause, we take the definition of the effect as the starting point to prove only the existence of the cause and some of its properties, while the quiddity of the cause remains unknown. This is what happens in the case of the separate substances.

Reply to 3.   Man's happiness is twofold. One is the imperfect happiness found in this life, of which the Philosopher speaks; and this consists in contemplating the separate substances through the habit of wisdom. But this contemplation is imperfect and such as is possible in our present life, not such that we can know their quiddity. The other is the perfect happiness of heaven, where we will see God himself through his essence and the other separate substances. But this happiness will not come through a speculative science; it will come through the light of glory.

Reply to 4.   As we have said, the speculative sciences are directed to an imperfect knowledge of the separate substances.

Reply to 5.   We are endowed with principles by which we can prepare for that perfect knowledge of separate substances but not with principles by which to reach it. For even though by his nature man is inclined to his ultimate end, he cannot reach it by nature but only by grace, and this owing to the loftiness of that end.[19]

---

[19] See *Summa Theol.* 1-2.5.5, ad 1[m]; *De Veritate* 22.7.

Appendix 1

The Division of the Sciences in St. Thomas' Commentary on the *Ethics*[1]

As the Philosopher says in the beginning of the *Metaphysics*,[2] it belongs to the wise man to put things in order. This is because wisdom is the highest perfection of reason, whose business it is to know order. For, although the sense powers know some things absolutely, it belongs to the intellect or reason alone to know the order of one thing to another.

Now there is a twofold order in things. One is the order of the parts of some whole or some multitude to each other, for example, the arrangement of the parts of a house among themselves. The other is the order of things to an end. And this order is more primary than the former one; for, as the Philosopher says in the *Metaphysics*,[3] the order of the parts of an army among themselves depends on the order of the whole army to its leader.

Now order is related to reason in four different ways. There is an order that reason does not make but simply examines; for example, the order of natural things. There is another order that reason by its thinking produces in its own activity; for example, when it establishes order among its concepts and the signs of its concepts, for they are meaningful sounds. The third order is that which reason by its thinking produces in the acts of the will. And the fourth order is that which reason by its thinking makes in the exterior things that it produces, as in the case of a box or a house.

---

[1] *In I Eth.* lect. 1, ed. Leonine, pp. 3-4.
[2] Aristotle, *Metaphysics* 1.2, 982a18.
[3] Aristotle, ibid., 12.10, 1075a14-16.

Now, because rational thinking is perfected through a scientific habit, there are different sciences corresponding to the different orders that it is the office of reason to consider. The *philosophy of nature* is concerned with the order of things that human reason examines but does not make, so that we also include both mathematics and metaphysics under the philosophy of nature.[4] The order that reason by its act of thinking produces in its own act pertains to *rational philosophy*, which is concerned with the order of the parts of discourse to each other and the order of principles to conclusions. The order of voluntary actions belongs to the consideration of *moral philosophy*. And the order that reason by its thinking produces in external things, made through human reason, pertains to the *mechanical arts*.

Appendix 2

Metaphysics as a Science: Introduction to St. Thomas' Commentary on the *Metaphysics*[1]

As the Philosopher teaches in his *Politics*,[2] when several things are directed to one end, one of them must be director or ruler and the

---

[4] St. Thomas here refers to the current division of the sciences (of Stoic origin) into natural, rational, and moral philosophy, with metaphysics included under natural philosophy. As far as I know, he does not mention this division elsewhere. St. Bonaventure adopts this division in his *De Reductione Artium ad Theologiam*, in *Opera Omnia* (Quaracchi, 1891), 5: 320-321. For the Stoic tripartite division of the sciences, see Diogenes Laertius, *Lives of Eminent Philosophers*, 7, 40, 41, vol. 2, p. 151. For the inclusion of mathematics under physics, see ibid. 132, p. 237.

[1] *In Meta.* Prooemium, ed. Cathala-Spiazzi, pp. 1-2. I am grateful to James P. Reilly, the editor of the forthcoming Leonine edition of the Commentary on the *Metaphysics*, for the opportunity to consult the critical Latin text for this translation of the Prologue.

[2] Aristotle, *Politics* 1.5, 1254a30.

rest directed or ruled. This is evident in the union of soul and body, for the soul naturally commands and the body obeys. The same is also true among the powers of the soul, for according to the natural order the irascible and concupiscible powers are ruled by reason.

Now all the sciences and arts are directed to one end, namely to the perfection of man, which is his happiness. So it follows that one of them must be the ruler of all the rest; and this science rightly claims the name of wisdom, for it belongs to the wise man to direct others.

Furthermore, if we carefully examine how someone is suited to rule, we can know which science this is and the sort of objects it studies. For just as men of strong intellect are by nature rulers and masters of others, while those robust in body and weak in mind are by nature subjects, as the Philosopher says in the above-mentioned work,[3] so the science that is most intellectual should be naturally the ruler of the others; and this is the science that treats of the most intelligible beings.

Now "the most intelligible beings" can be understood in three ways. First, from the point of view of the degree of knowing. Clearly, that from which the intellect derives its certainty seems to be the more intelligible being. Consequently, since the intellect acquires certitude in science from causes, the knowledge of causes seems to be intellectual in the highest degree. It also follows that the science treating of first causes seems to be the supreme ruler of the others.

Second, "the most intelligible beings" can be understood by comparing the intellect with the senses. Sense knowledge is of the particular, whereas the intellect seems to differ from the senses in that it comprehends universals. That science, then, is supremely intellectual that treats of the most universal principles. These are

---

[3] Ibid., 1254b15ff.

APPENDIX 2

97

being and the properties that accompany being as such, e.g., one and many, potency and act. Principles of this kind should not remain completely unstudied because without them it is impossible to have a full knowledge of what is proper to any genus or species. Nor should they be studied in any one particular science; since they are needed for a knowledge of every genus of beings, with equal reason they would be investigated in every particular science. It follows, then, that principles of this kind are studied in one universal science, which, being supremely intellectual, is the ruler of the others.

Third, "the most intelligible beings" can be understood from the viewpoint of the intellect's own natural condition. Because anything has intellectual capacity owing to its freedom from matter, those things must be supremely intelligible that are most disengaged from matter. For the intelligible object and the intellect must be proportionate to each other and belong to the same genus, since the intellect and the intelligible object are one in act. Now those things are most separated from matter that abstract not only from individual matter (such as natural forms understood universally, which are the objects of natural science), but entirely from sensible matter; and these are separated from matter not only in thought, like mathematicals, but also in existence, such as God and the Intelligences. Consequently, the science inquiring into these beings seems to be most intellectual and the director or mistress of the rest.

Now this threefold consideration is not to be attributed to different sciences but to one.[4] For the above-mentioned separated

[4] The one science of metaphysics investigates the first and universal causes of being, being-in-general, and God. It is not divided into ontology or the study of being-in-general, and rational theology or the study of the existence and nature of God. This division was proposed by Christian Wolff (1679-1754); to these divisions of metaphysics he added rational psychology, whose object is the soul, and cosmology, whose object is the world in general. See E. Gilson and T. Langan,

substances are the universal and primary causes of being. What is more, it belongs to the same science to investigate the proper causes of any genus and the genus itself, as for example natural philosophy investigates the principles of natural bodies. So it must belong to the same science to investigate the separated substances and being-in-general (*ens commune*), which is the genus[5] of which the above-mentioned substances are the common and universal causes.

Furthermore, it is evident from what has been said that although this science is concerned with the three objects mentioned, nevertheless it does not concern just any one of them as its subject, but only being-in-general. For the subject in a science is that whose causes

---

Modern Philosophy. Descartes to Kant, pp. 172-180; J. Owens, *An Elementary Christian Metaphysics*, pp. 7-8. The Wolffian division of metaphysics had a profound effect on Neoscholasticism. See J. Owens, "Theodicy, Natural Theology, and Metaphysics," *The Modern Schoolman* 28 (1957), 127, nn. 3, 5. An example of this influence is found in F. Van Steenberghen, *Epistemology*, trans. M. J. Flynn, pp. 288-290.

The statement that metaphysics has being (*ens*) for its subject must be understood in the light of St. Thomas' notion of being. This is not identical to the Aristotelian notion. See J. Owens, *The Doctrine of Being in the Aristotelian 'Metaphysics,'* 3rd ed., p. 309; E. Gilson, *Le Thomisme*, 6th ed., p. 186. For St. Thomas, a being (*ens*) is anything that has being (*esse*). See *In XII Meta.* lect. 1, ed. Cathala-Spiazzi, n. 2419. By *esse* he means the act of existing (*actus essendi*), which he regards as the deepest and most intimate principle in things, in virtue of which they exist. Thus in St. Thomas' view the subject of metaphysics is eminently existential, since metaphysics investigates being primarily from the perspective of the act of existing. See G. B. Phelan, "A Note on the Formal Object of Metaphysics," in *Selected Papers*, pp. 63-66; idem, "The Existentialism of St. Thomas," ibid., pp. 67-82; E. Gilson, *Being and Some Philosophers*, pp. 154-189. Metaphysics as a whole is directed to a knowledge of the first cause of the existence of things, namely God. See *Summa contra Gentiles* 3.25.

[5] Being is not a genus in the strict sense of the term. (See *In III Meta.* lect. 8, n. 433). It is here called a genus because it is the subject of metaphysics and hence analogous to the subject-genera of the other sciences. For the subject-genus of a science, see *In I Post. Anal.* lect. 15, nn. 3-4.

and properties we investigate, but not the causes themselves of any genus under inquiry. For the knowledge of the causes of any genus is the end attained by the inquiry of the science. However, even though the subject of this science is being-in-general, the whole science is said to concern what is separate from matter both in existence and in thought. For not only are those things called separate in existence and thought that can never exist in matter, like God and the intellectual substances, but also those that can be without matter, such as being-in-general. This, however, would not be possible if they depended on matter for their existence.

This science, then, is given three names corresponding to the three objects mentioned above, from which its perfection is derived. It is called *divine science* or *theology* inasmuch as it treats of the substances referred to above. It is called *metaphysics* because it considers being and its attendant properties; for these objects that go beyond physics are discovered by the process of analysis as the more universal is discovered after the less universal. And it is called *first philosophy* inasmuch as it considers the first causes of things.

We have now explained the subject of this science, its relation to the other sciences, and how it is named.

Appendix 3

The Order of Learning the Sciences

1.   The ultimate happiness of man consists in his most excellent activity, and this belongs to his highest power, the intellect, in regard to the best intelligible object, as the Philosopher says in the *Ethics*.[1]

---

[1] Aristotle, *Nicomachean Ethics* 10.7, 1177a12-22.

Now, since an effect is known through its cause, it is clear that a cause is more intelligible in its nature than an effect; although sometimes, as far as we are concerned, effects are better known than causes, because we take our knowledge of universal and intelligible causes from the particular things that fall under the senses.

Absolutely speaking, therefore, the first causes of things must be in themselves the greatest and best of intelligible objects, because they are the greatest beings and the truest things, since they are the cause of the essence and truth of other beings, as the Philosopher explains in the *Metaphysics*.[2] But these primary causes are less well known and later known as far as we are concerned. For our intellect is related to them as the owl's eye is to the light of the sun, which it cannot see perfectly owing to its extreme brightness. Consequently, the ultimate happiness that man can have in this life must consist in the contemplation of the first causes; for the little that can be known about them is more lovable and excellent than everything that can be known about lesser things, as is clear from the Philosopher in the *De Partibus Animalium*.[3] And it is through the completion of this knowledge in us after the present life that man is made perfectly happy, according to the words of the Gospel: *This is eternal life, that they may know thee, the only true God.*[4]

So the principal aim of the philosophers was that, through all their investigations of things, they might come to know the first causes. That is why they placed the science concerned with first causes last, and allotted the final period of their lives to its consideration. They began first of all with logic, which teaches the method of the sciences. Second, they went on to mathematics, which even boys

[2] Aristotle, *Metaphysics* 2.1, 993b26-31.
[3] Aristotle, *De Partibus Animalium* 1.5, 644b31-35.
[4] John 17:3.

are capable of learning. Third, they advanced to the philosophy of nature, which requires time because of the needed experience. Fourth, they proceeded to moral philosophy, of which a young person cannot be a suitable student. And finally they applied themselves to divine science, whose object is the first causes of things.

> St. Thomas, *In Librum de Causis*,
> lect. 1, ed. Saffrey, pp. 1-2.

2.   [Aristotle] raises the question why a boy can become a mathematician but cannot become wise, that is to say a metaphysician or physicist, in other words a natural philosopher.[5] His reply to this, as far as the philosophy of nature is concerned, is that mathematical entities are known by abstraction from sensible things, which are the objects of experience, and as a result a great length of time is not needed to grasp them. The principles of natural things, however, which are not separated from sensible things, are known through experience, for which much time is needed.

As far as wisdom is concerned, he adds that the young do not believe, that is, do not understand with their mind, things pertaining to wisdom or metaphysics, though they may speak them with their lips. But the nature of mathematical entities is not obscure to them, because their definitions concern things that can be imagined, whereas the objects of metaphysics are purely intelligible. Now the young can easily grasp what falls under the imagination, but they

---

[5] Aristotle, *Nicomachean Ethics* 6.8, 1142a16. For a discussion of this question, see E. Gilson, *Thomas Aquinas and our Colleagues*. For a different view of the teaching of metaphysics, see G. Klubertanz, "St. Thomas on Learning Metaphysics," *Gregorianum* 35 (1954), 3-17; idem, "The Teaching of Thomistic Metaphysics," ibid., pp. 187-205. On this subject, see J. Wippel, *Metaphysical Themes in Thomas Aquinas*, pp. 95-102.

cannot understand with their mind whatever goes beyond sense and imagination, for their minds are not yet vigorous and trained to such reflections because of the shortness of their lives and the many physical changes they are undergoing.

So the proper order of learning will be the following. First, boys should be instructed in logical matters, because logic teaches the method of the whole of philosophy. Second, they are to be instructed in mathematics, which does not require experience and does not transcend the imagination. Third, they should be trained in the natural sciences which, though not transcending sense and imagination, nevertheless require experience. Fourth, they are to be instructed in the moral sciences, which require experience and a soul free from passion, as is said in the first book.[6] Fifth, they should be taught matters concerning wisdom and divine science, which go beyond the imagination and require a vigorous mind.

> St. Thomas, *In VI Eth.* lect. 7, ed.
> Leonine, vol. 47^2, pp. 358-359.

[6] Aristotle, ibid., 1.3, 1095a4-9.

Bibliography

A. ANCIENT AND MEDIEVAL AUTHORS

Albert the Great. *De Vegetabilibus et Plantis.* In *Opera Omnia,* vol. 10. Ed. A. Borgnet. Paris, 1890-1899.

Aristotle. *Aristoteles Graece ex recensione Immanuelis Bekkeri.* Ed. Academia Regia Borussica, Berlin, 1831-1870.

————. *Aristotle's Metaphysics, a Revised Text with Introduction and Commentary.* Ed. W. D. Ross. Oxford, 1924.

————. *The Basic Works of Aristotle.* Ed. R. McKeon. New York, 1941.

Augustine. *De Civitate Dei.* CSEL, vol. 40; CCL, vol. 47.

————. *De Doctrina Christiana.* PL, vol. 34; CCL, vol. 32.

————. *De Genesi ad Litteram.* CSEL, vol. 28.

————. *De Trinitate.* PL, vol. 42; CCL, vol. 16.

Averroes. *Aristotelis Stagiritae Libri Omnes ... cum Averrois Cordubensis Variis in Eosdem Commentariis.* Venice, 1574.

————. *Commentarium Magnum in Aristotelis de Anima Libros.* Ed. F. S. Crawford. Cambridge, Mass., 1953.

Avicenna. *Avicenna Latinus, Liber de Anima seu Sextus de Naturalibus.* 3 vols. Ed. S. Van Riet. Louvain-Leiden, 1968-1980.

————. *Avicenna Latinus, Liber de Philosophia Prima sive Scientia Divina.* Ed. S. Van Riet. 2 vols. Louvain-Leiden, 1977-1980.

————. *Avicennae Arabum Medicorum Principis Canon Medicinae.* Venice, 1608.

————. *Opera Philosophica.* Venice, 1508. Reprint: Frankfurt, 1961.

Boethius. *De Consolatione Philosophiae.* CSEL, vol. 67.

————. *De Trinitate.* PL, vol. 64.

————. *In Isagogen Porphyrii Commenta.* CSEL, vol. 48.

————. Selection from the Second Commentary on the *Isagoge* of Porphyry. Trans. R. McKeon. In *Selections from Medieval Philosophers*, vol. 1. New York, 1929.

————. *The Theological Tractates and the Consolation of Philosophy.* Ed. and trans. H. F. Stewart, E. K. Rand and S. J. Tester. The Loeb Classical Library. Cambridge, Mass., 1973.

Bonaventure. *De Reductione Artium ad Theologiam.* In *Opera Omnia*, vol. 5. Quaracchi, 1891.

Cajetan, Thomas de Vio. *The Analogy of Names, and the Concept of Being.* Trans. E. A. Bushinski, with H. J. Koren. Pittsburgh, 1953.

————. *De Nominum Analogia.* Rome, 1934.

————. *In De Ente et Essentia D. Thomae Aquinatis Commentaria.* Turin, 1934.

Cicero. *Tusculanae Disputationes.* Ed. and trans. J. E. King. Loeb Classical Library. London-Cambridge, Mass., 1950.

Diogenes Laertius. *Lives of Eminent Philosophers.* Ed. R. D. Hicks. 2 vols. London-New York, 1925.

Dionysius, Pseudo-. *Dionysiaca, recueil donnant l'ensemble des traductions latines des ouvrages attribués au Denys de l'Aréopage.* Paris, 1937.

————. *On the Divine Names and the Mystical Theology.* Trans. C. E. Rolt. London, 1920.

————. *Opera.* PG, vol. 3.

Gilbert of Poitiers. *The Commentaries on Boethius.* Ed. N. Häring. Toronto, 1966.

Gregory the Great. *Moralia.* PL, vols. 75-76.

Hugh of St. Victor. *Didascalion de Studio Legendi.* Ed. C. Buttimer. Washington, DC, 1939.

————. *The Didascalion of Hugh of St. Victor.* Trans. J. Taylor. New York, 1961.

John of St. Thomas. *Cursus Philosophicus Thomisticus*, vol. 1: *Ars Logica.* Turin, 1930.

Kilwardby, Robert. *De Ortu Scientiarum.* Ed. Albert G. Judy. London-Toronto, 1976.

[*Liber de Causis.*] *Book of Causes.* Trans. D. J. Brand. Niagara Falls, NY, 1981.

————. *Die pseudo-aristotelische Schrift "Über das reine Gute" bekannt unter dem Nomen "Liber de Causis."* Ed. O. Bardenhewer. Freiburg-i.-B., 1882.

Liber de Spiritu et Anima (Alcher of Clairvaux?) PL 40.

Paterius. *Liber de Expositione Veteris et Novi Testamenti.* PL, vol. 79.

Peter of Auvergne. Commentary on Book 3 of the *Meteors.* In St. Thomas Aquinas, *Opera Omnia,* ed. Leonine, vol. 3. Rome, 1886.

Plato. *The Dialogues of Plato.* Trans. B. Jowett. 2 vols. New York, 1937.

————. *Opera.* Ed. J. Burnet. Oxford, 1902-1906.

Porphyry. *Isagoge.* In *Commentaria in Aristotelem Graeca,* 4.1. Berlin, 1887.

————. *Isagoge.* Trans. E. W. Warren. Toronto, 1975.

Ptolemaeus, Claudius. *Syntaxis Mathematica.* Teubner edition. Leipzig, 1878.

Thomas Aquinas. *Opera Omnia.* Ed. Leonine, Rome, 1882–. Vol. 3: *Commentaria in libros De Caelo et Mundo.* Vol. 2: *Commentaria in libros Physicorum.* Vol. 1: *Commentaria in Perihermenias; Commentaria in libros Posteriorum Analyticorum.* Vol. 40: *De Substantiis Separatis.* Vol. 22: *De Veritate.* Vol. 43: *Opuscula. De Operationibus Occultis Naturae; De Judiciis Astrorum; De Ente et Essentia.* Vol. 47: *Sententia libri Ethicorum.* Vols. 13-15: *Summa contra Gentiles.* Vols. 4-12: *Summa Theologiae.*

————. *Commentarium in librum De Anima.* Ed. A. M. Pirotta. Turin-Rome, 1959.

————. *Expositio in Epistolam ad Romanos.* In *Opera Omnia,* ed. S. E. Fretté, vol. 20. Paris, Vivès, 1876.

————. *Expositio in libros Metaphysicorum.* Ed. M. R. Cathala and R. M. Spiazzi. Turin, 1950.

————. *Expositio super librum Boethii De Trinitate.* Ed. B. Decker. Leiden, 1955; reprint, slightly corrected, 1959.

————. *In Boetium De Trinitate Expositio.* Ed. P. Uccelli. Rome, 1880.

————. *In Librum Boethii De Trinitate, Quaestiones Quinta et Sexta.* Ed. P. Wyser. Fribourg-Louvain, 1948.

————. *Le "De Ente et Essentia," texte établi d'après les manuscrits parisiens.* Ed. M. D. Roland-Gosselin. Le Saulchoir, Kain, 1926.

————. *Quaestiones Disputatae.* Rome, 1942. Vol. 1: *De Potentia Dei.*
   Vol. 2: *De Spiritualibus Creaturis.* Vol. 3: *De Veritate.*
————. *Scriptum super libros Sententiarum Magistri Petri Lombardi.* Ed.
   P. Mandonnet (vols. 1, 2) and M. F. Moos (vols. 3, 4). Paris,
   1929-1947.
————. *Summa contra Gentiles.* Leonine manual ed. Rome, 1934.
————. *Summa Theologiae.* Latin and English edition. 60 vols. New
   York-London, 1964-1966.
————. *Super Librum de Causis Expositio.* Ed. H. D. Saffrey. Fribourg-
   Louvain, 1954.
————. *Tractatus de Substantiis Separatis.* Ed. and trans. F. J. Lescoe.
   West Hartford, Conn., 1963.
————. *Aristotle's De Anima in the Version of William of Moerbeke and
   the Commentary of St. Thomas Aquinas.* Trans. K. Foster and S.
   Humphries. London, 1951.
————. *Aristotle on Interpretation.* Trans. J. T. Oesterle. Milwaukee, 1962.
————. *Basic Writings of St. Thomas.* Trans. A. C. Pegis. 2 vols. New
   York, 1945.
————. *Commentary on Aristotle's Physics.* Trans. R. J. Blackwell, et
   al. New Haven, Conn., 1963.
————. *Commentary on the Metaphysics of Aristotle.* Trans. J. P. Rowan.
   2 vols. Chicago, 1964.
————. *Commentary on the Nicomachean Ethics.* Trans. C. I. Litzinger.
   2 vols. Chicago, 1964.
————. *An Introduction to the Metaphysics of St. Thomas Aquinas.* Texts
   selected and trans. by J. F. Anderson. Chicago, 1953.
————. *The Letter of Saint Thomas Aquinas De Occultis Operibus Naturae
   ad Quemdam Militem Ultramontanum.* Trans. J. B. McAllister.
   Washington, DC, 1939.
————. *On Being and Essence.* Trans. A. Maurer. 2nd ed. Toronto, 1968.
————. *On Spiritual Creatures.* Trans. M. C. Fitzpatrick. Milwaukee,
   1949.
————. *On the Truth of the Catholic Faith (Summa contra Gentiles).*
   Trans. A. C. Pegis, J. F. Anderson, V. J. Bourke and C. O'Neil.
   5 vols. New York, 1955-1957.

————. *The Pocket Aquinas.* Selections from the writings of St. Thomas, ed. V. J. Bourke. New York, 1960.

————. *Questions on the Soul.* Trans. J. H. Robb. Milwaukee, 1984.

————. *The Trinity and the Unicity of the Intellect.* Trans. Sister Rose Brennan. St. Louis, 1946.

————. *Truth.* Trans. R. W. Mulligan, et al. 3 vols. Chicago, 1952-1954.

B. Modern Works Cited and General Reading

Allers, Rudolf. "On Intellectual Operations." *The New Scholasticism* 26 (1952), 1-36.

Anderson, James. *The Bond of Being. An Essay on Analogy and Existence.* St. Louis, 1949.

Chenu, M. D. "Arts 'mécaniques' et œuvres scrviles." *Revue des sciences phil. et théol.* 29 (1940), 313-315.

————. "La date du commentaire de S. Thomas sur le *De Trinitate* de Boèce." *Revue des sciences phil. et théol.* 30 (1941-1942), 432-434.

————. *Is Theology a Science?* Trans. A. H. N. Green-Armytage. New York, 1959.

————. "Notes de lexicographie philosophique médiévale: *Disciplina.*" *Revue des sciences phil. et théol.* 25 (1936), 686-692.

————. *La théologie comme science au XIIIᵉ siècle.* 3rd ed. Paris, 1969.

————. Toward Understanding Saint Thomas. Trans. A. M. Landry and D. Hughes. Chicago, 1964.

Choisnard, Paul. *Saint Thomas d'Aquin et l'influence des astres.* Paris, 1926.

Collins, James. *The Thomistic Philosophy of the Angels.* Washington, DC, 1947.

Compton, John. "Reinventing the Philosophy of Nature." *The Review of Metaphysics* 33 (1979), 3-28.

Congar, Yves. *Thomas d'Aquin. Sa vision de théologie et l'Église.* Variorum reprint. London, 1984.

Connolly, F. G. "Abstraction and Moderate Realism." *The New Scholasticism* 27 (1953), 72-90.

————. "Sciences vs. Philosophy." *The Modern Schoolman* 29 (1952), 197-209.

Crombie, A. C. *Augustine to Galileo. The History of Science A.D. 400-1650.* London, 1952. 2nd ed.: *Medieval and Early Modern Science.* 2 vols. New York, 1959.

————. *Robert Grosseteste and the Origins of Experimental Science 1100-1700.* Oxford, 1953.

Cunningham, F. "A Theory of Abstraction in St. Thomas." *The Modern Schoolman* 35 (1958), 249-270.

Decker, B. "Corrigenda et Addenda à l'édition du 'In Boethium de Trinitate' de s. Thomas d'Aquin." *Scriptorium* 13 (1959), 81-82.

Deferrari, R. and Sister M. Inviolata Barry. *Lexicon of St. Thomas Aquinas Based on the Summa Theologica and Selected Passages in his Other Works.* Washington, DC, 1948.

De Koninck, Charles. "The Unity and Diversity of Natural Science." In *The Philosophy of Physics,* ed. V. E. Smith, pp. 5-24. Jamaica, NY, 1961.

Deman, Th. "Notes de lexicographie philosophique médiévale: *Probabilis.*" *Revue des sciences phil. et théol.* 22 (1933), 260-290.

Dondaine, H. F. "Cognoscere de Deo 'quid est'." *Recherches de théologie ancienne et médiévale* 22 (1955), 72-78.

Duhem, Pierre. *Le système du monde. Histoire des doctrines cosmologiques de Platon à Copernic.* 10 vols. Paris, 1913-1954.

Elders, Leo. *Faith and Science. An Introduction to St. Thomas' Expositio in Boethii de Trinitate.* Rome, 1974.

Finance, Joseph de. *Être et Agir dans la philosophie de saint Thomas.* Paris, 1945.

Gardeil, P. "La 'certitude probable'." *Revue des sciences phil. et théol.* 5 (1911), 237-266, 441-485.

Geiger, L. B. "Abstraction et séparation d'après s. Thomas. *In de Trinitate,* q. 5, a. 3." *Revue des sciences phil. et théol.* 31 (1947), 3-40.

Gils, P.-M. "Notes on the Reprint of Decker's Edition of St. Thomas' *In Boethium De Trinitate.*" In *Bulletin Thomiste* 11 (1960-1961), no. 54, pp. 41-44.

Gilson, Etienne. *Being and Some Philosophers.* 2nd ed. Toronto, 1952.
————. *The Christian Philosophy of St. Thomas Aquinas.* Trans. L. K. Shook. New York, 1956.
————. *Constantes philosophiques de l'être.* Paris, 1983.
————. *The Elements of Christian Philosophy.* Garden City, NY, 1960.
————. *Réalisme thomiste et critique de la connaissance.* Paris, 1947.
————. *Thomas Aquinas and our Colleagues.* Princeton, 1953. Reprinted in *A Gilson Reader,* ed. A. C. Pegis, pp. 278-297. New York, 1957.
————. *Le Thomisme.* 6th ed. Paris, 1965.
————. *The Unity of Philosophical Experience.* New York, 1937.
————, and Thomas Langan. *Modern Philosophy. Descartes to Kant.* New York, 1963.
Grabmann, Martin. *Die theol. Erkenntnis- und Einleitungslehre des hl. Thomas von Aquin auf Grund seiner Schrift "In Boethium de Trinitate."* Freiburg in der Schweiz, 1948.
Grant, Edward, ed. *A Source Book in Medieval Science.* Cambridge, Mass., 1974.
Haskins, Charles H. *Studies in the History of Mediaeval Science.* Cambridge, Mass., 1924. 2nd ed. New York, 1960.
Heath, Thomas. *Mathematics in Aristotle.* Oxford, 1949.
Henle, Robert. *Method in Metaphysics.* Milwaukee, 1951.
Isaac, J. "La notion de dialectique chez saint Thomas." *Revue des sciences phil. et théol.* 34 (1950), 481-506.
Jaeger, Werner. *Aristotle. Fundamentals of the History of His Development.* Trans. R. Robinson. Oxford, 1934.
Jaki, Stanley L. "Maritain and Science." *The New Scholasticism* 58 (1984), 267-292.
————. *The Relevance of Physics.* Chicago, 1966.
Kane, William. "Abstraction and the Distinction of the Sciences." *The Thomist* 17 (1954), 43-68.
Kibre, Pearl. *Studies in Medieval Science: Alchemy, Astrology, Mathematics, and Medicine.* London, 1984.
Klubertanz, George. "St. Thomas on Learning Metaphysics." *Gregorianum* 35 (1954), 3-17.

————. "The Teaching of Thomistic Metaphysics." Ibid., pp. 187-205.

Leroy, M. V. "Le savoir spéculatif." *Revue Thomiste* 48 (1948), 236-339. Contains "'Abstractio' et 'separatio' d'après un texte controversé de saint Thomas," pp. 328-339. Reprinted in *Jacques Maritain, son œuvre philosophique*, pp. 236-339. Paris, 1949.

Lindberg, D. C., ed. *Science in the Middle Ages*. Chicago, 1978.

Litt, Th. *Les corps célestes dans l'univers de saint Thomas d'Aquin*. Louvain-Paris, 1963.

McInerny, Ralph M. *The Logic of Analogy*. The Hague, 1961.

McKeon, Richard. "Rhetoric in the Middle Ages." *Speculum* 17 (1942), 1-32.

McMullin, Ernan. "Compton on the Philosophy of Nature." *The Review of Metaphysics* 33 (1979), 29-58.

————. "Is There a Philosophy of Nature?" *Proceedings of the International Congress of Philosophy*, Vienna 1968, 4: 295-305.

————. "Philosophies of Nature." *The New Scholasticism* 43 (1969), 29-74.

Mariétan, Joseph. *Problème de la classification des sciences d'Aristote à s. Thomas*. Paris, 1901.

Maritain, Jacques. *Art and Scholasticism and the Frontiers of Poetry*. Trans. J. W. Evans. New York, 1962.

————. "The Conflict of Methods at the End of the Middle Ages." *The Thomist* 3 (1941), 527-538.

————. *Distinguish to Unite: or, The Degrees of Knowledge*. Trans. under the supervision of G. B. Phelan. New York, 1959.

————. *The Dream of Descartes*. Trans. M. L. Andison. New York, 1944.

————. *Existence and the Existent*. Trans. L. Galantière and G. B. Phelan. New York, 1948.

————. *An Introduction to Philosophy*. Trans. E. I. Watkin. London, 1930.

————. *Philosophy of Nature*. Trans. I. Byrne. New York, 1951.

————. *A Preface to Metaphysics*. New York, 1939.

————. *Quatre essais sur l'esprit dans sa condition charnelle*. Paris, 1956.

————. *Réflexions sur l'intelligence et sur sa vie propre*. Paris, 1924.

————. *Science and Wisdom*. Trans. B. Wall. London, 1940.

————. "Sur la doctrine de l'aséité divine." *Mediaeval Studies* 5 (1943), 39-50.

Maurer, Armand. "Form and Essence in the Philosophy of St. Thomas." *Mediaeval Studies* 13 (1951), 165-176.

————. "A Neglected Thomistic Text on the Foundation of Mathematics." *Mediaeval Studies* 21 (1959), 185-192.

Mendoza, C. A. L., and J. E. Bolzan. "Santo Tomas y los metodos de las ciencias especulativas." *Sapientia* 27 (1972), 37-50.

Merlan, Philip. "Abstraction and Metaphysics in St. Thomas' *Summa*." *Journal of the History of Ideas* 14 (1953), 284-291.

Meyerson, Emile. *De l'Explication dans les sciences*. Paris, 1921.

Moody, Ernest A. *Studies in Medieval Philosophy, Science, and Logic: Collected Papers 1933-1969*. Berkeley, 1975.

Neumann, S. *Gegenstand und Methode der theoretischen Wissenschaften nach Thomas von Aquin auf Grund der* Expositio super librum Boethii De Trinitate. Beiträge zur Geschichte der Philosophie und Theologie des Mittelalters 41.2. Münster, 1965.

Nogar, Raymond. "Toward a Physical Theory." *The New Scholasticism* 25 (1951), 397-438.

Owens, Joseph. "Analogy as a Thomistic Approach to Being." *Mediaeval Studies* 24 (1962), 303-322.

————. "Aquinas on Knowing Existence." *The Review of Metaphysics* 29 (1976), 670-690.

————. *The Doctrine of Being in the Aristotelian 'Metaphysics'*. 3rd ed. Toronto, 1978.

————. *An Elementary Christian Metaphysics*. Milwaukee, 1963. Reprinted Houston, 1985.

————. *A History of Ancient Western Philosophy*. New York, 1959.

————. *An Interpretation of Existence*. Milwaukee, 1968. Reprinted Houston, 1985.

————. "Metaphysical Separation in Aquinas." *Mediaeval Studies* 34 (1972), 287-306.

————. "Theodicy, Natural Theology, and Metaphysics." *The Modern Schoolman* 28 (1951), 126-137.

Paetow, L. J. *The Arts Course at Mediaeval Universities with Special Reference to Grammar and Rhetoric.* Urbana, 1910.

Paré, G., A. Brunet and P. Tremblay. *La renaissance du XIIe siècle. Les écoles et l'enseignement.* Paris-Ottawa, 1933.

Peghaire, Julien. *Intellectus et Ratio selon s. Thomas d'Aquin.* Paris, 1936.

Pegis, Anton C. "Penitus Manet Ignotum." *Mediaeval Studies* 27 (1965), 212-226.

Petrin, Jean. *Connaissance spéculative et connaissance pratique. Fondements de leur distinction.* Ottawa, 1948.

Phelan, Gerald B. "Being and the Metaphysicians." In *From an Abundant Spring; the Walter Farrell Memorial Volume of the Thomist,* pp. 423-447. New York, 1952. Reprinted in *Selected Papers,* ed. A. G. Kirn, pp. 41-62. Toronto, 1967.

————. "The Existentialism of St. Thomas." *Proceedings of the American Catholic Philosophical Association* 21 (1946), 25-40. Reprinted in *Selected Papers,* ed. A. G. Kirn, pp. 67-82. Toronto, 1967.

————. "A Note on the Formal Object of Metaphysics." In *Essays in Modern Scholasticism,* pp. 47-51. Westminster, MD, 1944. Reprinted in *Selected Papers,* ed. A. G. Kirn, pp. 63-66. Toronto, 1967.

————. *Saint Thomas and Analogy.* Milwaukee, 1941.

————. "Verum Sequitur Esse Rerum." *Mediaeval Studies* 1 (1939), 11-22. Reprinted in *Selected Papers,* ed. A. G. Kirn, pp. 133-154. Toronto, 1967.

Philippe, M. D. "Abstraction, addition, séparation dans la philosophie d'Aristote." *Revue Thomiste* 48 (1948), 461-479.

Rashdall, Hastings. *The Universities of Europe in the Middle Ages.* Ed. F. M. Powicke and A. B. Emden. 3 vols. Oxford, 1936.

Régis, L. M. "Analyse et synthèse dans s. Thomas." *Studia Mediaevalia* (Bruges, 1948), 303-330.

————. *Epistemology.* Trans. I. C. Byrne. New York, 1959.

————. "Un livre ... La philosophie de la nature. Quelques apories." In *Études et Recherches. Philosophie,* Cahier 1, pp. 127-156. Ottawa, 1936.

Robert, J. D. "La métaphysique, science distincte de toute autre discipline philosophique, selon saint Thomas d'Aquin." *Divus Thomas* 50 (Piacenza, 1947), 206-222.

Roberts, L. D., ed. *Approaches to Nature in the Middle Ages.* Binghamton, 1983.

Sarton, George. *Introduction to the History of Science.* 3 vols. Baltimore, 1927-1948.

Schmidt, Robert. *The Domain of Logic According to Saint Thomas Aquinas.* The Hague, 1961.

————. "L'emploi de la séparation en métaphysique." *Revue philosophique de Louvain* 58 (1960), 373-393.

Simmons, Edward. "In Defense of Total and Formal Abstraction." *The New Scholasticism* 29 (1955), 427-440.

————. "The Thomistic Doctrine of the Three Degrees of Formal Abstraction." *The Thomist* 22 (1959), 37-67.

Simon, Yves. *Critique de la connaissance morale.* Paris, 1934.

————. "Maritain's Philosophy of the Sciences." *The Thomist* 5 (1942), 85-102.

Smith, Gerard. *Natural Theology.* New York, 1950.

Smith, Vincent. "Abstraction and the Empiriological Method." *Proceedings of the American Catholic Philosophical Association* 26 (1952), 35-50.

————. *Philosophical Physics.* New York, 1950.

————. *St. Thomas on the Object of Geometry.* Milwaukee, 1954.

Steenberghen, Fernand Van. *Epistemology.* Trans. M. J. Flynn. New York-London, 1949.

Sweeney, Leo. *A Metaphysics of Authentic Existentialism.* Englewood Cliffs, NJ, 1965.

Taylor, F. Sherwood. *The Alchemists, Founders of Modern Chemistry.* New York, 1949.

Thorndike, Lynn. *A History of Magic and Experimental Science.* 8 vols. New York, 1923-1958.

Tonquédec, Joseph de. *Questions de cosmologie et de physique chez Aristote et saint Thomas.* Paris, 1950.

Van Ackeren, G. F. *Sacra Doctrina. The Subject of the First Question of the* Summa Theologiae *of Saint Thomas Aquinas.* Rome, 1952.

Van Riet, G. *Problèmes d'épistémologie.* Louvain, 1960.

————. "La théorie thomiste de l'abstraction." *Revue philosophique de Louvain* 50 (1952), 353-393.

Wallace, William A. *Causality and Scientific Explanation.* 2 vols. Ann Arbor, 1972-1974. Reprinted Washington, DC, 1981.

————. "St. Thomas's Conception of Natural Philosophy and its Method." In *Studi Tomistici. La philosophie de la nature de saint Thomas d'Aquin,* ed. L. Elders, pp. 7-27. Vatican City, 1982.

————. "Thomism and Modern Science: Relationships Past, Present, and Future." *The Thomist* 32 (1968), 67-83.

Weisheipl, James A. "Classification of the Sciences in Medieval Thought." *Mediaeval Studies* 27 (1965), 54-90.

————. *The Development of Physical Theory in the Middle Ages.* London-New York, 1959. Reprinted Ann Arbor, 1971.

————, ed. *The Dignity of Science. Studies in the Philosophy of Science Presented to William Humbert Kane,* OP (=*The Thomist* 24 [1961]). Washington, DC, 1961.

————. *Friar Thomas d'Aquino. His Life, Thought, and Work.* New York, 1974. 2nd ed. Washington, DC, 1983.

————. *Nature and Gravitation.* River Forest, Ill., 1955.

————. "The Nature, Scope and Classification of the Sciences." In *Science in the Middle Ages,* ed. D. C. Lindberg, pp. 461-482. Chicago, 1978.

————. "The Relationship of Medieval Natural Philosophy to Modern Science: the Contribution of Thomas Aquinas to Its Understanding." In *Science, Medicine and the Universities 1200-1550* (=*Manuscripta* 20 [1976]), pp. 181-196.

Wippel, John F. *Metaphysical Themes in Thomas Aquinas.* Washington, DC, 1984.

Zimmermann, Albert. *Ontologie oder Metaphysik? Die Diskussion über den Gegenstand der Metaphysik im 13. und 14. Jahrhundert.* Leiden-Köln, 1965.

Index

abstraction, meaning and modes of xviii-xxxi, 34-41; a way of knowing xviii n; degrees of xxiv; formal and total xxvii, xxviii; of a form, of a whole xx, xxi, xxiv, xxv, 37-41; different from separation 37; in mathematics xxi, 37-39, 41, 42; in the philosophy of nature xx, xxi, 28, 29, 41; in metaphysics xxii-xxxi, 41. *See also* separation.

addition, role of xxix, xxx.

agriculture 20, 22, 44.

Albert, St. xi.

alchemy 18, 22.

Allers, R. xxiv n.

analogy 84 n.

analysis (*resolutio*) xxxviii, 71, 72.

Anderson, J. 82 n, 84 n.

Andronicus of Rhodes 15 n.

Aristotle (The Philosopher), notion of science ix; divisions of theoretical sciences xv; doctrine of abstraction xxix-xxx; notion of essence xxx; primary philosophy 15; science deals with the necessary 28; optics, music, astronomy as branches of mathematics 43 n; distinction between dialectical and scientific arguments 59; and *passim*.

arithmetic 17 n, 44.

art 18; liberal arts xv, 17-19; mechanical arts 19 n.

astronomy (*astrologia*) xxxii, 11 n, 23, 43, 45, 46.

Augustine, St. 10, 19, 20, 26, 47, 62 n, 76.

Avempace 92.

Averroes (The Commentator) xxx n, 17, 47, 48, 53, 55, 65, 88 n, 89, 90, 92.

Avicenna 20, 21 n, 23, 50, 85, 88 n.

Bacon, Roger xi.

being, grasped in judgment xvii, xviii, 35 ; as terminus of analysis in the mental order 72.

being-in-general (*ens commune, ens inquantum ens*), subject of metaphysics xvii, xxii, 98, 99. *See also* metaphysics, subject of.

Boethius, division of theoretical sciences xv, xvi, 3, 5-7; their modes of procedure xxxii, 3, 4, 7, 8; vii, xxxii, xxxv, xli, 16, 24, 58, 60, 71, 74 n, 76, 87.

Bolzan, J. E. 58 n.

Bonaventure, St. 95 n.

Bourke, V. 58 n.

Brunet, A. 17 n.

Cajetan xxvii, xxviii.

certitude xxxv, xxxvi, 67-69.

Chenu, M.-D. vii n, 19 n, 52 n, 58 n, 60 n, 61 n.

individuals, as objects of science 27-29.
individuation, by matter 28, 29, 42.
intellectualiter, mode of procedure in
    metaphysics xxxii, 59.
intellectus 62, 63, 74.
intention, second 64 n, 70 n.
intermediate science (*scientia media*)
    xi, xv, xxxii, 43-46.
Isaac, J. 64 n.
Isaiah 62.

Jaeger, W. 15 n.
Jaki, S. L. x n.
John, St. 100 n.
John of St. Thomas xxvi, xxvii, 17 n,
    21 n, 64 n.
judgment: *see* composition and divi-
    sion.

Kane, W. xxviii n.
Kibre, P. ix n.
Kilwardby, Robert xxv n.
Klubertanz, G. 101 n.

Langan, T. 97 n.
Leroy, M.-V. xxviii n.
Liber de Causis 62 n.
Liber de Spiritu et Anima 60, 63, 76.
Litt, Th. 44 n.
logic (rational philosophy), instrument
    of science 16; teaches method of
    sciences xxxi, 17, 69, 70, 102 ; a
    liberal art 20 n; *logica docens, utens*
    63; subject of 69, 70, 95; studied
    first 69, 100, 102.

McAllister, J. 44 n.
McInerny, R. M. 84 n.
McKeon, R. 17 n.
McMullin, E. x n.

Mariétan, J. ix n.
Maritain, J. viii n, x n, xiii n, xv n,
    xviii n, xxiv, xxvii n, xxviii n,
    xxxii n, xxxvi n, xxxviii n, xxxix n,
    13 n, 15 n, 17 n-19 n, 23 n, 38 n,
    43 n, 64 n, 74 n, 77 n, 82 n, 84 n.
mathematics, abstraction in xxi, xxii,
    38, 39, 41-43; can be learned by the
    young 17, 18, 101; method of
    xxxv-xxxvii, 67-69; role of imagina-
    tion in xxxix, 78; subject of 14, 38,
    39, 42, 43; included under philoso-
    phy of nature 95; learned after logic
    100, 102.
matter, determinate (*signata*) 29; intel-
    ligible 38, 40, 42, 43; principle of
    individuation 28, 29, 42.
Maurer, A. xxx n, 27 n, 38 n.
medicine 18, 20, 21.
Mendoza, C. A. L. 58 n.
Merlan, P. xxiii n, xxviii n.
metaphysics, subject of xxii, 22, 52, 53,
    99; why so named 14, 15, 73, 99;
    first of the sciences 23; abstraction
    in xxii, xxiii, 41; uses the other
    sciences 23; gives principles to the
    other sciences 23, 24, 73; method
    of xxxvii, xxxviii, 70-73; how rela-
    ted to senses, imagination and intel-
    lect xxxix, xl, 76-79; also called first
    philosophy, theology or divine
    science 99; to be learned last 101,
    102.
method, of the philosophy of nature
    xxxiv, xxxv, 65, 66; of mathematics
    xxxv, xxxvi, 67-69; of metaphysics
    xxxvii-xl; specificity of scientific
    methods xxxii, 79; rational 63-66;
    learning 67-69; intellectual 70-73.
Meyerson, E. xiii.

abstraction in proper sense xx; mode of abstraction in metaphysics xxii, xxiv, xxv, 37, 41.
Sherwood, F. 18 n.
Simmons, E. xxviii n.
Simon, Y. 13 n.
Smith, G. 24 n.
Smith, V. E. x n, xxviii n, 38 n.
Steenberghen, F. van 98 n.
stoic division of science 95 n.
supposition xxxvi, xxxvii.
Sweeney, L. xxiv n.
synthesis (*compositio*) xxxviii, 71, 72.

theology, as name of metaphysics 14, 99; as taught in sacred Scripture viii, xv, xxiii n, 52, 53.
Thorndike, T. 18 n, 44 n.

Tremblay, P. 17 n.
trivium 17.

Uccelli, P. A. xxvi n.

Van Ackeren, G. F. 52 n.
Van Riet, G. xxviii n.
Varro 20.
virtues, intellectual 15, 16.

Wallace, W. A. ix n, x n.
Weisheipl, J. A. ix n, x n.
Wippel, J. F. xxiv n, 15 n, 23 n, 82 n, 101 n.
wisdom 16.
Wisdom, Book of 47.
Witelo xi.
Wolff, C. 97 n.